The *Naiṣkarmyasiddhi* of Sureśvara:

Sri Garib Dass Oriental Series No. 136

The *Naiṣkarmyasiddhi* of Sureśvara: A Monograph

John Grimes

Sri Satguru Publications
A Division of
Indian Books Centre
Delhi-India

Published by :
Sri Satguru Publications
Indological and Oriental Publishers
A Division of
Indian Books Centre
40/5, Shakti Nagar,
Delhi-110007
(INDIA)

First Edition : Delhi, 1992

ISBN 81-7030-317-6

Printed in India

S. K. Mehra at Mehra Offset Press, 1976, Chandni Mahal Darya Ganj,
New Delhi-110002

Professor R. Balasubramanian

TABLE OF CONTENTS

III. CHAPTER THREE - SAMUCCAYA

IV. CHAPTER FOUR - NATURE OF THE SELF

V. CHAPTER FIVE - INTERPRETATION OF MAHĀVĀKYA

VI. CHAPTER SIX - SCRIPTURE

VII. CHAPTER SEVEN - THE LOCUS OF AVIDYĀ

VIII. CHAPTER EIGHT - TRANSLITERATION OF THE NAIṢKARMYASIDDHI

PREFACE

The Advaita Vedānta sourcebook *sampradāya* (lineage) includes a class of independent expository works known as the *siddhi*-literature. These works differ from Advaita's primary source-books (*prasthāna-traya*) in that they set forth not only the essentials of Advaita but also present new facets by way of dialectics with other schools. Four works in this group have attracted more reknown than the others by virtue of their authoritative character as well as their polemics. These four are: Maṇḍana's *Brahmasiddhi*, Sureśvara's *Naiṣkarmyasiddhi*, Vimuktātman's *Iṣṭasiddhi*, and Madhusūdana Sarasvatī's *Advaitasiddhi*.

Advaita Vedānta tradition also acknowledges the *Naiṣkarmyasiddhi* for a second reason. As a compendium of Advaita philosophy, it touches on all the salient features of that system.[1] Consisting partly of verse and partly of prose, it presents a clear, brief, and simple account of the Advaita doctrine. Its style is charming and Sureśvara handles the philosophical arguments with ease.

The work is divided into 423 stanzas connected by a prose commentary and is divided into four chapters (of roughly 100 stanzas each). As well, it is important to the Advaita tradition for two

---

[1]Sureśvara himself describes it as such: *aśeṣa-vedāntasāra-saṅgraha-prakaraṇam* - *Naiṣkarmyasiddhi, sambandhokti* to I.1.

additional reasons. First, it was written by Sureśvara (who was allegedly a Mīmāṃsaka before his conversion to Advaita[2]). As a defence of Advaita doctrine against Mīmāṃsaka doctrine, it is a classic. Second, Sureśvara is known, respected, and honored in the Advaita tradition as part of the authoritative triumvirate: Vyāsa, Śaṅkara, and Sureśvara. This gives him and his works an importance as an authority which cannot be overlooked or overvalued.

The central question that the book deals with is 'liberation from transmigratory existence and the means thereto'. Ignorance of the Self (*Ātman*) is the

---

[2]Whether Sureśvara was Maṇḍanamiśra or not is a controversial issue up to this day. See *Śrī Śaṅkaravijaya of Anantānandagiri*, canto 55, Ed., N. Veezhinathan, University of Madras, 1971, p. 174; Cidvilāsa's *Śaṅkaravijayavilāsā* quoted in Introduction to *Ślokavārtika*, Madras University Sanskrit Series, No. 13, p. x; Guruvaṁśakāvya, Sri Vani Vilas Press, Srirangam, Canto II, 41-50, 59; *Śaṅkaradigvijaya*, Anandasrama Sanskrit Series, pp. 292-293; *Brahmasiddhi*, S. Kuppuswami, ed., Madras Government Oriental Manuscript Series, no. 4; M. Hiriyanna, "Sureśvara and Maṇḍanamiśra," *Journal of the Royal Asiatic Society of Great Britain and Ireland*, April 1923 and January 1924; S.K. Ramanatha Sastri, "Bhavabhuti and his identity," *The Journal of the Andhra Historical Research Society*, Rajahmundry, July 1926, vol. I, part 3, pp. 125-129; Ramakrishna Kavi, "Identity of Suresvara," *Journal of the Andhra Historical Research Society*, vol. V, part III, 1931, pp. 187-192; Suryanarayana Sastri, "Maṇḍana and Sureśvara," *The Journal of the Madras University*, vol. XI, No. 1, 1939, pp. 30-40.

cause of bondage and it can be removed only by right knowledge of the Self which is obtainable from *śruti* texts. The first chaper deals primarily with 'action versus knowledge' as the means to liberation. The second chaper focuses on the distinction between the Self and the not-Self. The third chapter discusses the locus and content of ignorance as well as subjecting the *śruti mahāvākyas* to a rigorous analysis. Finally, the concluding chapter summarises the first three chapters and quotes illustrative passages from the *Upadeśasāhasrī* and *Māṇḍūkyakārikā* in support of what he has previously stated.

There are a number of translations of the *Naiṣkarmyasiddhi:* M. Hiriyanna's *Naiṣkarmyasiddhi of Sureśvara with the Candrikā of Jñānottama,* A.J. Alston's *The Realization of the Absolute,* R. Balasubramanian's *The Naiṣkarmyasiddhi of Sureśvara.* This monograph differs from those in that it is an attempt to present a lucid account of Sureśvara's work by grouping the dialectics from various parts of the work into topical sections.

ACKNOWLEDGEMENTS

The *Naiṣkarmyasiddhi* was taught in the Master's program at the Radhakrishnan Institute for Advanced Study in Philosophy, University of Madras, for many years. The department has always been closely associated with Sureśvara's various works, beginning with Suryanarayana Sastri and continuing through T.M.P. Mahadevan to R.

Balasubramanian, and it was there that I learned to love Sureśvara. I would like to acknowledge my special indebtedness to Professor R. Balasubramanian for introducing me to, and teaching me the *Naiṣkarmyasiddhi*.

Thanks also must be extended to the University of Madras and the University of Lethbridge for providing me with the opportunity to learn, write, and refine this work.

I would also like to thank Sri Satguru Publications, a division of the Indian Books Centre and Naresh Gupta, the Director, for their assistance.

JOHN GRIMES
University of Lethbridge
Lethbridge, Alberta, Canada

NAIŞKARMYASIDDHI

CHAPTER ONE

I. CHAPTER ONE - NAIŞKARMYASIDDHI

I.i THE TITLE "NAIŞKARMYASIDDHI"

Sureśvara selected the title of this work from Śaṅkara's *Bhagavadgītā-bhāṣya.*[1] In Śaṅkara's commentary, the state of 'freedom from action and its influence' (*naiṣkarmya*) is described as equivalent to the state attained through renunciation (*sannyāsa*). This is a state in which one has transcended all actions (*karma*) through a proper and perfect knowledge of the Self (*Ātman*). It is the stage beyond all actions. Thus, Sureśvara wrote the *Naiṣkarmyasiddhi* to stand as a compendium containing the essence of the Upaniṣadic teachings regarding *Brahman,* action, and knowledge.

The initial prose portion introduces the idea of 'attainment' (*siddhi*) 'of a state wherein an individual is free from' (*naiṣ*) 'action' (*karma*) and all its influences. This is followed by the first verse which stands as a benedictory stanza, as well as an epitome of the teaching of the text as a whole.

---

[1]*Bhagavadgītābhāṣya XVIII.49. asaktabuddhiḥ sarvatra jitātmā vigataspṛhaḥ naiṣkarmyasiddhiṁ paramāṁ saṁnyāsenā 'dhigacchati*

I.ii OPENING PROSE PORTION

The *Naiṣkarmyasiddhi* opens with a *sambandhokti*, a prose portion which is traditionally employed in Indian philosophical works to introduce new ideas at the beginning of a verse or text. Advaitic tradition says that Sureśvara initially wrote the verses and then, at the insistence of some friends, wrote the prose portions to serve as a guide to understanding the verses. Thus, the entire work, as we know it today, is partly in prose and partly in verse.

In this opening prose section, Sureśvara discusses the causal chain of suffering. He says, "From the Creator on down, all living beings desire to avoid pain. . ."[2] He points out the various links in the karmic chain which culminate in the root-cause of suffering (*duḥkha*) - which is the non-apprehension of the Self (*Ātman*).

It is a truism to say that every living being desires to avoid pain. However, the primary cause of pain, or suffering, is the embodied condition which every living being finds himself or herself in. Further, action or *karma* is responsible for this embodied condition which cannot be escaped since it is rooted in one's previously amassed good and bad actions. This karmic law is an accepted, and fundamental, tenet of all Indian systems. As well, note that this karmic chain implies both that there is a necessary link between every event and its antecedent cause *and*, a possible freedom to ethically

[2]*Naiskarmyasiddhi*, Book 1, introduction. *ābrahmastamba-paryantaiḥ . . .*

advance. Not only does every deed produce its direct result of pleasure or pain, but it also establishes a tendency (*saṁskāra*) to repeat the same deed in the future.[3] The former aspect involves necessity while the latter, *viz.* tendencies, are under an individual's own control.

The links of the causal chain of suffering continue with: desire (*rāga*) and aversion (*dveṣa*).[4] They are responsible for the above mentioned, previously performed, collected actions. In turn, a false superimposition (*adhyāsa*) is responsible for desire and aversion.[5] An uncritical acceptance of duality, which is but a non-enquiry (*avicāra*) into the nature of Reality, is responsible for this false superimposition. The mistaking of the Real for the unreal and the unreal for the Real rests upon a primary, and foundational, ignorance of the non-dual Self - even as the fancied water of a mirage rests upon an individual's ignorance of the nature of the desert. Why does an individual see a mirage and not the sand of the desert? Because one does not *know* that 'it' is merely sand and not water. The mistake is due to a wrong impression caused by: an ignorance of the real nature of the object; a predisposition to see the unreal; a mistaken impression; and favorable conditions.

---

[3] These are technically known as the '*phala*' and the '*saṁskāra*'.

[4] Ibid., "*karmaṇaś ca rāga-dveṣāpadatvād rāga-dveṣayoś ca...*"

[5] In his *Brahmasūtrabhāṣya*, Śaṅkara defines superimposition as '*atasmin tad buddhiḥ*) - the cognition of something as something else. See Śaṅkara's *Adhyāsa bhāṣya* '*adhyāso nāmo atasmimstadbuddhiḥ ity avocāma*'.

Since ignorance of the non-dual Self is the cause of an individual's pain, one's aim should be to remove this ignorance (*avidyā/ajñāna*). This is to be accomplished by an enquiry into the nature of the Self. Even as light is the only remedy for the removal of darkness, so too, knowledge is the only eradicator of ignorance. The light of correct knowledge is the only dispeller of the darkness of ignorance. No amount of actions can remove the illusory water superimposed upon the desert's sand. There never was water there; there never will be water there; nor is there water there now. To remove this wrong impression, all that is required, and all that will be successful, is solely the light of right knowledge.

Action, which is the result of ignorance, cannot hope to destroy its parent and source. The delusive cognition of the not-Self cannot be removed by darkness which is its cause.[6] Pain is the result of being embodied; being embodied is the result of previously acquired merit and demerit; merit and demerit are the result of action; action is dependent upon desire/aversion; desire and aversion are superimpositions; superimposition is caused by non-enquiry; non-enquiry is the result of ignorance. Hence, ignorance is the sole and root cause of suffering and can be removed only by knowledge.[7]

The primary interest and over-riding concern of the *Naiṣkarmyasiddhi* is this topic, i.e., showing the

---

[6] *Naiṣkarmyasiddhi* I.24 *"ajñāna-hāna-mātratvān mukteḥ karma na sādhanam karmāpamārṣṭi nājñānaṃ tamasīvotthitaṃ tamaḥ"*

[7] Ibid., I. Introduction *"ajñāna-nivṛtteśca samyag-jñāna..."*

how of *Brahman*-knowledge. Its emphasis is on an enquiry into, and an analysis of, whether it is by knowledge alone or by action or action-cum-knowledge that liberation (*mokṣa*) is achieved. Philosophically speaking, this point touches the heart of Advaita. ***Brahma-bhāva*** is ***sva-bhāva*** - Experience of the Absolute is experience of the Self. Liberation is not something alien to oneself, to be imported or created anew. It is one's very essence. The light is within, only one should see.

There are those (Mīmāṃsakas) who advocate that liberation is a product of action and those (Brahmadatta, Maṇḍana) who advocate it is a product of action-cum-knowledge. However, in any form, action which is a product of ignorance, cannot destroy its source. Thus, 'right-knowledge' (*samyag-jñāna*), according to Jñānottama, is different from: meditation (*upāsanā*); erroneous cognitions (*jñāna-ābhāsa*) - whether they be pseudo-knowledge-generated or empirical-knowledge-generated (*vyāvahārika pramāṇa*); or action (*karma*).

This is not to say that Advaitins do not recognize the usefulness of action. Though action does not produce liberation, still, actions must be performed until the rise of knowledge. There is an Upaniṣadic text, "*Brahmins* seek to realize *Brahman* through the study of the *Vedas*, through sacrifices, through gifts, and through austerity and fasting."[8] Through this performance (of action) there arises a purity enabling an individual to become eligible for

---

[8]*Bṛhadāraṇyaka Upaniṣad* IV.iv.22 *"tam etaṁ vedānuvacanena brāhmaṇā vividiṣanti yajñena dānena, tapasānāśakena".*

a true enquiry into *Brahman*. Sureśvara says that actions subserve knowledge only through the channel of purification. Thus, though actions are not the proximate aid to liberation (*antaraṅga-sādhana*), they are the remote auxiliaries (*bahiraṅga-sādhana*). More of this later.

Returning to Jñānottoma's commentary, he says that *upāsanā*, in a technical sense, means to meditate upon something as something else (as enjoined by Scripture), i.e., one should meditate upon the *praṇava 'Om'* as *'Ātman'*.[9] All worldly knowledge, as well as all action, is dependent upon, and presupposes, duality. Since ignorance is nothing more than mistaking multiplicity for the Reality, it is obvious that anything which partakes of, and is dependent upon, multiplicity cannot remove its source (i.e., ignorance).

The aim of an individual is to remove ignorance. The method to be employed is an earnest enquiry. The result to be obtained is right knowledge. And right knowledge arises only from the Scripture (*śruti*).[10] However, to say that Scripture is the basic authority for Advaita does not mean that the Advaitin is a strict fundamentalist, a dogmatist, or a literalist. It does not imply a 'blind acceptance of' or 'unthinking belief in', the words of the *Veda*. Words are not mere isolated sounds. They convey meaning and this meaning must be understood. The emphasis here is placed upon their purport. If a

---

[9]*Muṇḍaka Upaniṣad* II.2.6 *"aum ity evaṁ dhyāyathātmānam"*.

[10]See *Bṛhadāraṇyaka Upaniṣad* III.9.26 *"taṁ tvā aupaniṣadam puruṣam pṛcchāmi"*; Also *Brahmasūtra* I.1.4 *'tat tu samanvayāt'*.

text is accepted without a proper enquiry, or if its meaning is only superficially understood, the consequences will not yield the fruits intended. Reasoning is both helpful and necessary in understanding the teaching of the Scripture. It is true that the Absolute is beyond reasoning and ungraspable by thoughts or through words. Nevertheless, reasoning is useful, in a negative way, in so far as it can assure the individual as to what is not real. As well, language is useful and beneficial in indicating the nature of the Absolute even if 'words fail to reach'.

Valid knowledge is described as of two kinds: that which relates to the empirical reality and that which relates to the Absolute Reality.[11] No other means of knowledge, excepting Scripture, can impart knowledge of supra-sensible facts. This is mere common sense. Perception and all the other empirical means of knowledge are limited to the empirical world (by definition). Since all the things in the phenomenal world possess certain fixed characteristics such as grossness, fineness, etc., name and form are their warp and woof. But the non-dual Reality is trans-empirical, trans-sensual, free from all such distinctions.

Jñānottama's second elucidation points out that right knowledge excludes every kind of erroneous cognition (*jñāna-ābhāsa*). These include both valid empirical cognitions as well as erroneous ones. His

---

[11] *Vedāntaparibhāṣā* ch. 7, pp. 150-151 *"evam nirūpitānām pramāṇānām prāmāṇyamdvividham,vyāvahārikatattvāvedakatvam pāramārthikatattvāveda-katvanccheti"*.

third point is one that Sureśvara never tires of stating again and again, implicitly and explicitly, namely, that ignorance can never be removed by means of action. Thus, the aim of the work is to remove ignorance by means of an enquiry which will yield right knowledge.

I.iii THE ESSENCE OF THE WORK

The first verse, which stands as an invocation to secure the fulfillment of the work, contains the essence of the entire treatise implicitly. It alludes to how the entire universe comes into existence from the non-dual *Brahman*.

khānilāgnyabdharitryantaṃ
sṛakphaṇīvodgatam yataḥ dhvāntacchide
namastasmai haraye buddhisākṣiṇe[12]

So much Advaitic thought is packed into this verse! Sureśvara, in citing the well-known rope-snake example, introduces, in cryptic form, the Advaitin's theory of transfiguration or apparent change (*vivarta-vāda*). Simply put, this theory of causation states that the world is but an illusory appearance superimposed by ignorance upon the non-dual *Brahman*. The cause, *Brahman*, is real and ever remains the same (Sureśvara's garland) while

---

[12]*Naiṣkarmaysiddhi* I.1. "Reverence to the Lord, the kDestroyer of darkness and Witness of the intellect, from Whom the world consisting of the five elements has come forth in mere appearance - like the snake which appears to exist in a garland."

the effect, the world, (Sureśvara's snake) is unreal being but an illusory superimposition of ever-changing names and forms. The substratum (*adhiṣṭhāna*), whether it be *Brahman* or a garland, never changes even though a universe of multiplicity or an individual snake is superimposed thereon. In actuality, there never was a world/snake there, nor will there ever be, nor is there now.

Advaita Vedānta is unique in stating that any reference to a theory of creation or causality is not intended to expound creation or causality, but merely to demonstrate the one non-dual Reality. The 'creation-texts' (*sṛṣṭi-vākya*) allude to the universe, not to teach creation or how causality works, but solely to culminate in conveying the non-dual *Brahman*.

> As food, too, is an offshoot, seek after its root, *viz.*, fire. And as fire is an offshoot, seek after its root, *viz.*, Being (*Sat*).[13]

Gauḍapāda said,

> If creation is represented by means (of the similes of) clay, iron, sparks, and other things, that is only a means for making it understand

---

[13]*Chāndogya Upaniṣad* VI.viii.4; "*tasya kva mūlaṁ syād anyatrānnāt, evam eva khalu, saumya, annena śuṅgenāpo mūlam anviccha. . .*" Quoted by Śaṅkara in his *Brahmasūtrabhāṣya* I.iv.14 p. 273.

> that (in reality) there is no difference whatever.[14]

According to Advaita, the universe is not said to be created. It is only the way in which *Brahman* appears under the limiting conditions of space and time. As an appearance, the universe is but a projection of *Brahman* as invested with names and forms.

Vivarta-vāda affirms that the effect pre-exists in the cause in the sense that it is the cause which appears as the effect. The effect is nothing new - it is only the cause 'appearing' differently. Ordinarily, two things or events are said to be in a causal relation when one of them produces or brings about the other. The cause is the one which produces and the effect is what is produced. The cause is said to be different from the effect and prior to it. As well, in any process of causation, three aspects are involved: the material, instrumental, and efficient causes.

A causal relation ordinarily implies that one event or thing 'causes' another. Advaita maintains that such a position is riddled with inconsistencies. Within the Indian philosophical tradition, two views of causation are maintained: Either the effect is pre-existent in the cause (*satkāryavāda*) or else the effect is non-existent in the cause prior to its production (*asatkāryavāda*).

The basic position of those who hold that the effect is a *de novo* creation from the cause

---

[14]*Maṇḍūkyakārikā* III.15. *"mṛllahovisphulinkhādhyaiḥ sṛṣṭiryā coditā' nyathā upāyaḥ so'vatāraya nāsti bhedaḥ kathamcana."* Quoted by Śaṅkara, ibid.

(*asatkāryavādins*) contend that if such were not the case, causation itself would be rendered meaningless. If the effect is said to be 'pre-existent in the cause', then the question logically arises as to the necessity for its production **again**? Following this logic, the cause and its effect must differ and the effect must be non-existent before its production by the cause.

However, this position raises two fundamental problems. First, the cause and effect relation in regards to the material cause is unsatisfactory. Nothing can come out of something unless it is already (pre-)existent in that something. If such were not the case, then it would amount to disclaiming the need for a material cause for the production of an effect. A clay pot is dependent upon the material clay for its existence. And secondly, if the efficient cause is separate from the material cause, then this implies a limitation upon its Creator. For instance, God, as the efficient cause, would be bound to work upon material independent of Himself. Furthermore, He would be limited to creating only those forms which this given material would admit of.

Those who hold that the effect is pre-existent in the cause (*satkāryavādins*), maintain that such must be the case for otherwise, if the effect is not pre-existent in the cause, anything could come out of anything - and then only sometimes. There would be no determinative cause for a specific effect. Milk could come out of sand, and then, only sometimes.

In rebuttal, their opponents object that if the effect pre-exists in the cause, why does it need to be produced? Though this appears as a redundancy, *satkāryavādins* reply that the effect is not in the cause as such - it is latent in the cause and has to be brought out. Thus, what was latent must become patent.

However, still difficulties persist. Is the cause wholly transformed, or only a part of it, in the causal process? If the whole cause is transformed, then the cause ceases to be, and what happens to the cause in which the effect is said to pre-exist? And, if only a part of the cause changes into the effect, with the other part maintaining its substance, it will be like killing one-half of a chicken to eat and trying to keep the other half to lay eggs with.

The *satkāryavādins* reply to this objection by claiming that what is meant in saying that the cause is transformed into the effect is that what was not previously manifested is now made manifest. The clay as cause does not disappear when the pot as effect is produced. What was the cause, is now the effect, persisting in it.

However, still the dialectics continues. The opponent asks, what exactly does this 'manifestation' mean? The *satkāryavādin* is caught between the horns of another dilemma. Either one must admit that causation is redundant or else that it is impossible. And so it goes - with each theory of causation destroying the other's position. If the effect is already existent, it is redundant to say that the already-existent is created. If the effect is non-existent, it can never be produced. Either alternative fails to satisfy the demands of logic. Thus it is that the Advaitin propounds a doctrine of non-origination.[15] The universe is not a *de novo* creation, nor a transformation of something - but the appearance of *Brahman* under certain limiting adjuncts. Like every appearance, the world is not real (because, to the enlightened individual, it ceases to exist in its multiplicity). But, it is not unreal (for it appears to the senses). Being neither real nor unreal, it can only be said to be non-real or *mithyā/sadasatvilakṣaṇa, anirvacanīya*.

Advaita's (provisional) theory of causation implies six requisites:

1) There is a relation in terms of succession in the cause-effect relationship. The cause is always earlier and the effect is always later.
2) The relationship between the cause and the effect is an irreversible relationship. The cause always precedes the effect and never *vice-versa*.
3) The relationship between the cause and the effect is a necessary relationship and not a contingent one.
4) Cause and effect are not completely identical nor are they totally different. (If any two entities are absolutely different, they are not related by cause and effect, and if they are absolutely identical, then they are the same entity).
5) The relationship between cause and effect is a one-sided relationship. The effect is

[15]*Vivartavāda* was spoken of as *ajātivāda* (theory of non-origination) by Gauḍapāda in his *Māṇḍūkyakārikā* IV.5 *"khyāpyamānāmajātim..."*.

always dependent upon the cause and never *vice-versa.*

6) Between the cause and the effect, the cause alone is real.

These requisites logically lead to the discovery that any theory of causation is impossible. From the seeming reality of a causal relationship at an empirical level, one is led to the discovery that, philosophically speaking, there cannot be a logical causal relationship. An empirical practicality and appearance does not necessarily translate into a metaphysical reality.

By applying the above criteria to the famous rope-snake example of the Advaitins, the comprehension and implications of *vivartavāda* will become clear. The rope is the cause of the snake in the sense that the snake pre-existed (so to speak) in the rope. It is only the rope that appeared as the snake. The snake had its origin in the rope. It was sustained by the rope, and finally disappeared back into the rope. All the time, there was nothing else present than the rope. The rope never ceased being a rope, even while it appeared to the deluded individual as a snake. This is the very essence of the idea - a thing appearing differently without ceasing to be itself even during the different appearance.

Vivartavāda may be said to imply the central teaching of Advaita. This is cryptically summed up in the saying: The Absolute is real; the world is non-real; the individual and the Absolute are not different.[16] Or again, the central teaching of Advaita

---

[16] *Brahma satyam, jagan mithyā, jīvo brahmaiva nā 'paraḥ.*

is conveyed in the verse, 'The individual and the Absolute are one.'[17]

The first verse of the *Naiṣkarmyasiddhi* conveys this oneness even in its benedictory stanza.

> '*Hari*', the Lord, is in apposition to 'the witness of the intellect'. The Lord is not somewhere else, above and beyond. *Hari* is within the individual, here and now.[18]

I.iv. MAIN PURPOSE OF THE WORK (VERSES 2-8)

According to Sureśvara, he wrote this treatise to: 1) obey his teacher's command, 2) expound *jīva-brahma aikya*, 3) show that knowledge of the Self destroys ignorance, 4) become clearer on the doctrine, and 5) expound the essential nature of the Self.

Sampradāya or tradition plays a role within Advaita philosophy which cannot be over-emphasized. Advaita Vedānta, as one of the orthodox (*āstika*) schools of Indian philosophy, traces its origins to the *Vedas* - an origin which is lost in the mists of time. All Advaitins acknowledge their lineage in a familiar *śloka*:

---

[17] *Jiva brahma aikya.*

[18] *Naiṣkarmyasiddhi* I.1. *dhvāntacchide namastasmai haraye buddhisākṣiṇe*

Narāyanam Padmabhuvam Vasiṣtam
Saktinca tatputra Parāsaramca
Vyāsam Sukam Gauḍapādam mahāntam
Govinda yogīndramathāsya siṣyam
Srī Śaṅkarācāryamathāsya
Padmapādamca
Hastāmalakamca siṣyam
Tamtrotakam vārtikakāramanuyānasmad
Gurūnt santata mānatosmi

From the divine Lord Narāyana, the first teacher, up to Śuka, the son of Vyāsa, the line of succession is from father to son. As well, the lineage up to Śuka is clouded in the mists of history, myth, and legend. From Gauḍapāda onwards, the succession is no longer regarded as either divine or semi-divine, but now rests in the hands of human monks. Continuing up to today, this tradition exists in an unbroken line. From teacher to disciple, the teaching has been passed down the annals of time. Thus, within Indian philosophy, tradition and modernity meet - but never has tradition been discarded or delegated to an inferior role.

The point to be conveyed is that Sureśvara offers reverence to his teacher (*guru*)[19] in order to show: 1) that his tradition has an ancient and requisite authority, 2) that he is obedient to his teacher's command instructing him to expound the Upaniṣadic doctrine,[20] and 3) there are no defects in this work because his preceptor is authoritative.[21] Sureśvara wrote the book, not out of any desire for

---

[19]Ibid., I.2. *"garīyase namas. . ."*
[20]Ibid., I.3. *". . .guru-anuśikṣayā".*
[21]Ibid., I.5. *"gurunaiva vedārthasya. . ."*

personal name, fame, or gain, but only to further his own understanding, and if necessary, to correct any defects in his knowledge.[22]

The subject-matter of the treatise (*viṣayam prakaraṇam*) concerns the essential nature of the Self (*Ātman*).[23] The Self is said to be the innermost Reality. For instance, an analysis of the five sheaths (*pañca koṣa viveka*) which covers the Self reveals that the Self persists in all the five sheaths even while they vary and undergo change. Such an analysis reveals that what is grosser and more external and less pervasive is less real than what is subtler and more internal and more pervasive. This analysis reveals that the Self is the subtlest, inmost being, and therefore the most real. From the physical body, which is the grossest sheath, to the subtlest sheath of enjoyment there is to be found both impermanence and objectification. But the knower of all these sheaths is the subtlest, most pervasive of all. Even when all the objective elements are removed from the five sheaths, what remains is pure Consciousness, awareness, the *Ātman*. Even to say that nothing remains after dismissing all objective names and forms requires a consciousness which witnesses the absence of any name and form. This subtlest element of all is the witnessing Consciousness which is incapable of being negated.

---

[22]Ibid., I.6. *"na khyāti lābha pūjārthaṃ grantho'smābhir udīryate sva bodha pariśuddhyarthaṃ brahma vinnikaṣāśmasu"*.

[23]Ibid., I.4. *"yat-siddhāv idamaḥ siddhir yad-asiddhau na kiṃcanapratyag-dharmaika-niṣṭhasya yāthātmyaṃ vakṣyate sphuṭam"*

Thus, Sureśvara says, 'when the Self exists, the entire world exists'. 'If the Self is non-existent, all else will be non-existent'. This type of reasoning is called the method of co-presence and co-absence (*anvaya-vyatireka*). Sureśvara takes recourse to it in order to demonstrate that the Self, which is of the nature of Consciousness, is constant and necessary and therefore real, while the phenomena which constitute the world are inconstant, contingent, and therefore non-real. If the Self can be established, all else can be established. But, if the Self cannot be established, nothing else can be established.

According to Advaita, epistemologically speaking, all things are known or cognized because of the mind. Any act of perception involves the *tripuṭī* - the cognizer, the cognized, and the act of cognition. From the cognizer (*cidābhāsa*), which is a reflection of consciousness residing in the intellect, arises a valid means of knowledge (*pramāṇa*) which is a modification of the internal organ (*antaḥkaraṇa vṛtti*). The consciousness, upon reaching the object, assumes the form of that object. the modification is the transformation of the internal organ and connects the cognizer with the object cognized. This is possible because ignorance has obscured the omnipresent, intelligent Self and transformed itself into the world of diverse kinds.

The *cidābhāsa* is a reflection of Consciousness in the internal organ. Without the functioning of the mind or the internal organ, no knowledge will arise. Pure Consciousness alone will not give rise to empirical knowledge. This conclusion can be demonstrated by employing Sureśvara's above-mentioned use of the method of *anvaya-vyatireka.*

The four states of Consciousness - waking (*jagrat*), dreaming (*svapna*), deep sleep (*suṣupti*), and the fourth (*turīya*) show that the mind must function in order for determinate knowledge to arise. The first three states are mutually exclusive of one another. When an individual is awake, one is neither dreaming nor asleep. The same holds true in regards to both dreaming and deep sleep also. But the state of *turiya* is unique in that it persists in and underlies the other three.

In the waking state, the mind functions due to the reflection of Consciousness in it. The same holds true in regards to the dreaming state. In the deep sleep state, there is no definite knowledge of objects because the mind is not functioning. Only Consciousness is present and this is demonstrated by an individual's exclamation upon waking. 'I slept well' or 'I do not remember anything last night'.

This sense of 'I' is present throughout the three states, even though the three states are exclusive to one another. This personal identity which is established in the three states referring them all to the same individual is Consciousness. This 'I', which bears witness to the three states, is an awareness which underlies them. It is called the 'witness consciousness' (*sākṣi caitanya*). It is omnipresent in one's consciousness and makes for one's sense of self-identity. In actuality, it is a non-dual condition without any subject-object distinctions. It is the experience *par excellence.* It is the expansive

Consciousness which is ever-present - regardless of whether the mind or objects are present or not.

All this goes to show that the three states are not ultimate. They are transcended by *turiya,* which is ever-present. Thus, the plurality that is reflected in these three states is not the final truth. Even though the stillness of deep sleep gives a foretaste of the abiding Consciousness, it too must be transcended.

> Here is a clear statement of the true nature of the inner reality whose sole function is to exist as the witness and support of all. The existence and manifestation of all this world depends on its existence. If it did not exist, nothing would.[24]

The subject-matter of the book concerns the nature of the Self. Verse seven mentions four elements of the subject-matter which should be differentiated: *Anārtha* or suffering, (which, according to Sureśvara, is an effect of the failure to apprehend the Self); *anārtha hetu* or the cause of suffering (i.e., ignorance); *puruṣārtha* or the goal of life[25] (i.e., liberation or *mokṣa*); and *puruṣārtha hetu* or the means to obtain the goal of life (i.e., knowledge of the Self or *atmajñāna*).

---

[24]Ibid. (my translation)

[25]Four main values of life (*puruṣārthas*) are generally accepted in Indian philosophy: wealth (*artha*), enjoyment (*kāma*), righteousness (*dharma*), and liberation (*mokṣa*). The first is an economic value; the second is a psychological value; the third is a moral value; and the fourth is a spiritual value. The first two are secular values and the latter two are spiritual values.

Ignorance (*avidyā*) is called the seed of bondage and the cause of empirical existence. It binds one to the wheel of birth and death. Its cause is the failure to realize that one's own Self is the sole reality. Not only does it conceal the real nature of the Self, but it also projects the non-real world of multiplicity upon it. Both the content and locus of ignorance is the pure Self.[26] Upon its destruction (*avidyā-nāsa* or *avidyā-nivṛtti*), liberation arises. Enlightenment is not something to be newly obtained, but merely the removal of ignorance. As Maṇḍana said, "Liberation is the setting of ignorance."[27] White cloth is already white. It is the contingent adjunct of dirt which makes it appear black. In order to make the cloth white again, one need not add whiteness to it. It will be enough to merely wash the dirt away.

As was mentioned previously, *Brahman*-knowledge obtained through the Vedānta texts is the means to attain the goal of life. Sureśvara employs the analogy of fire in saying that it is the 'fire of knowledge which burns away the ignorance of the Self'.[28] Action cannot destroy ignorance for action is not opposed to it. Action is not only dependent

---

[26]According to Sureśvara (and the Vivaraṇa school), the content and locus of *avidyā* is *Brahman*. According to the Bhāmatī school, the locus of *avidyā* is the individual (*jīva*). See Chapter Three for a detailed discussion of this subject.

[27]See *Brahmasiddhi*.

[28]Compare: *Chāndogya Upaniṣad* V.xxiv.3 - All his evils are burnt just as the soft fibres of the *isika* reed would burn, when thrown into a fire. *Bhagavadgītā* IV.37 - As the fire which is kindled reduces all fuel to ashes, O Arjuna, so does the fire of knowledge reduce all *karmas* to ashes.

upon ignorance, but is, in fact, a product of ignorance.

Knowledge has been compared to fire. The analogy is apt for when fire burns an object, ashes are left over. So too, when the fire of knowledge burns the actions-in-store (*sañcita karmas*) and the actions-yet-to-come (*āgāmi karmas*), what is left over are the accumulated effects of past deeds which have begun fructify with the creation of one's present body (*prārabdha karmas*). These actions are only destroyed when their force is spent. They can neither be averted, avoided, or changed either by knowledge or grace.

Thus, while knowledge is said to remove the first two types of *karma*, *prārabdha karmas* must be experienced. This is explained by relating it to the action of a rotating fan. Even after the power of the fan has been turned off, the fan continues to rotate until its accumulated force has been spent. In a similar manner, even though knowledge burns the actions-which-are-yet-to-come, the actions which are giving impetus to the present incarnation must be experienced. It is in this sense that the Advaitin claims that a liberated-while-living-in-a-body (*jīvanmukta*) individual, is 'in the world, though not of the world'. The diversity of the world may continue to appear to the enlightened individual, even as the sun continues to appear to move across the sky though one is convinced that the sun is in reality, stationary. Pleasure and pain may continue to be experienced, yet to the *jīvanmukta*, neither really matters anymore. There is 'no one' there to be affected. Once the Self has been realized, multiplicity loses its reality.

> Where verily there is, as it were, a duality, there one knows another. But when to the Knower of *Brahman* everything has become the Self, what should one know and through what? Through what should one know That owing to which all this is known - through what, O Maitreyi, should one know the Knower?[29]

---

[29] *Bṛhadāraṇyaka Upaniṣad* II.4.14 *"yatra hi dvaitam iva bhavati, tad itara itaraṁ jighrati. . ."*.

CHAPTER TWO

II.i. INTRODUCTION

The over-riding concern, as well as the central topic, of the *Naiṣkarmyasiddhi* is to determine whether liberation (*mokṣa*) is to be attained by knowledge or by action. Traditionally the *Vedas* have been divided into two sections according to subject-matter: knowledge-section (*jñāna-kāṇḍa*) and action-section (*karma-kāṇḍa)* It is precisely at this juncture that our controversy arises. Both the Mīmāṃsaka and Advaitic traditions claim a common end in view, i.e., to lead individuals to liberation. The Mīmāṃsaka claim posits that this is to be achieved through action and the Vedāntins put forth knowledge as the path to liberation.

In this context, knowledge means knowledge of *Brahman*. It is the immediate intuition of the non-difference of the individual from *Braḥman*. This is dealt with particularly in the *Upaniṣads*. Tradition claims that the rest of the *Vedas* deal primarily with rites, duties, and moral laws, in short, the action-section. Without stretching the issue, a certain unity can be found between the two sections in that both propose to lead an individual from the temporal to the eternal. As well, Śaṅkara said, "The section of the *Vedas* dealing with knowledge has the same import as that dealing with rites."[1] The ques-

[1] See Śaṅkara's Commentary on the *Bṛhadāraṇyaka Upaniṣad* IV.4.22.

tion is: Is knowledge primary or is action primary or are they mutually efficient?

According to Advaita, actions, rites, and duties are preparatory to that *Brahman*-knowledge whereby liberation is attained. Actions purify the mind and prepare it for the liberating knowledge which is to come. On the other hand, both Pūrva Mīmāṃsā schools maintain the primacy of action - though they are split over the question as to whether there is such a think as knowledge of the Self or not.[2]

Even the Mīmāṃsakasadmit that action is the cause of bondage. However, they do not admit or agree to the claim that all actions should be relinquished. Only certain actions such as those which are desire-prompted (*kāmya*) or prohibited (*pratisiddha*) should be abstained from. But an individual should never give up the performance of obligatory (*nitya*) or occasioned (*naimittika*) actions.[3] Their reasoning is: just as sin or negative karmic consequences results from the performance of prohibited actions, so too, will sin result from the non-performance of obligatory rites. According to Mīmāṃsa, the *Vedas* are one's authority and as such prescribe what one should do and prohibit what one should not do. Thus the issue becomes one of interpretation or exegesis.

---

[2]The Bhāṭṭa school maintains that there is such a thing as knowledge of the Self, but that it is not needed in order to obtain liberation. The Prabhākara school claims that there is no such thing as knowledge of the Self at all.

[3]*Naiṣkarmyasiddhi* I.10.

There are six orthodox Indian philosophical systems that accept the authority of the *Veda*.[4] The *Pūrvamīmāṃsāsūtra* begins *'athāto dharma jijñāsa'* - 'now therefore, an enquiry into *dharma* and the *Uttaramīmāṃsāsūtra* begins, *'athāto brahma jijñāsa'* - 'now therefore, an enquiry into *Brahman'*.[5] Of these two, the Pūrva Mīmāṃsā upholds action and stresses the teaching contained in the earlier portions of the *Veda*, especially the *Brāhmaṇas*. Advaita Vedānta maintains that knowledge is the sole means to liberation and stresses the latter portions of the *Veda, viz.*, the *Upaniṣads*.

According to the Pūrva Mīmāṃsā school, the essence of the Scripture is injunctions and commandments which tell what ought-to-be-done (*vidhi*) and what ought-not-to-be-done (*niṣedha*). The be all and end all of the *Veda* is ritual injunctions. "Other texts are authoritative only in so far as they help the individual to action."[6] Thus, any descriptive information which may occur in the Scripture derives its meaningfulness only from the imperative statements therein. By themselves, existential statements are meaningless and have no independent logical status. It is only as complements of

---

[4]The six *āstika* schools (Nyāya, Vaiśeṣika, Sāṅkhya, Yoga, Pūrva Mīmāṃsā, and Uttara Mīmāṃsā or Vedānta) all accept the authority of the *Vedas*, though the two Mīmāṃsās especially emphasize this aspect.) However, Mīmāṃsā and Vedānta are devoted specially to an exposition of the Vedic texts. Both systems emphasize an investigation (*mīmāṃsā*) into the true import of the *Vedas*.

[5]*Pūrvamīmāṃsāsūtra* I.1.1 and *Brahmasūtra* I.1.1.

[6]*Mīmāṃsāsūtra I.2.1*. This refers to the well-known division of the *Veda* into *vidhi-vākya* (injunctions) and *artha-vākya* (existential passages).

injunctions that such passages gain meaning (for the Scripture need not say anything about an existent entity - as such things can readily be perceived and are not therefore in need of the Scripture). The Scripture, according to Mīmāṃsā, is there to point out the goal and to describe how to reach it. Its purpose is to inform individuals about what one should and should not do. Knowledge of existential things is in no way conducive to this end. Therefore, the Mīmāṃsakas contend that action alone will lead one to heave and, for this purpose, the Scripture exists.

Advaita, on the other hand, maintains that the purport of the Scripture is not to command something to be done, but to point to certain self-evident truths.[7] It is an obvious fact that the Scripture is composed of both types of passages: those which purport action as well as passages which are descriptions of existing states of affairs.

The Mīmāṃsakas declare that, by themselves, descriptive texts are meaningless. One need not do anything, nor can one do anything in regards to an established fact. However, the Advaitins reply that words cannot fail to reveal their meanings no matter to what purpose they are being employed. Some meaning is being conveyed and thus a statement is not entirely meaningless. Action is not the only bestower of meaningfulness. A descriptive statement conveys knowledge and since knowledge removes ignorance, it is gratuitous to declare that knowledge about an established fact is meaningless.

---

[7] See *Brahmasūtrabhāṣya* I.1.4.

For instance, the knowledge that what was mistaken for a snake is only a rope puts an end to one's fears - which is definitely a purportful result.

The Mīmāṃsaka claim that 'any sentence which does not have its purport in action is thereby a mere statement of something which can be known by one of the other valid means of knowledge' is not necessarily true. There is no necessary reason that an established entity must be perceived by perception, etc. Perceptibility, etc. is not the criterion for an established fact existing prior to being known. An established fact may be imperceptible or unknowable by a valid means of knowledge due to its being either extremely subtle or lacking in distinguishing marks. In fact the Advaitin asks, "How can that by which all the *pramāṇas* are established, be itself established by a *pramāṇa*?"[8]

In the Indian context, injunctive statements (*vidhi-vākya*) presuppose the achievement of various sorts of results as well as the recognition of an agent thereof while existential statements (*siddhārtha vākya*) are declarations of facts and statements whose subject-matter exists already. In actuality, these two types of statements have no real logical relation to each other. Both types of statements are no doubt valid within their given contexts. But what must be kept clearly in mind is the distinct subject-matter of each type of statement.

Injunctive statements are valid with regards to actions. Existential statements are valid with regards to facts. Both types of passages inform an

---

[8] *Brahmasūtrabhāṣya* II.1.4.

individual of something which that individual did not know before hand and could not have known otherwise. Thus, both types of passages function to make something known. Neither type of passage actually functions to produce activity. If, upon hearing either type of passage, one is desirous of performing some action, it is the desire that does the prompting and not the statement itself. The aim of the passage is to make something known, though what the two types of passages make known is entirely different. One may perform an action, not perform an action, or perform the action differently, according to one's individual whim, but in regards to a fact, there is nothing to be done.

It is in this context that Advaita makes a distinction between 'knowledge' which is object-dependent (*vastu-tantra*) and 'action' which is person-dependent (*puruṣa-tantra*). The former relates to knowledge of a thing as-it-is. There is nothing to do about it. As ignorance about an object disappears, knowledge of it arises on its own accord. On the other hand, the results of action are of four kinds: That which is produced (*utpādyam*), that which is attained (*prapāyam*), that which is modified (*vikār y a m*), and that which is purified (*saṁskāryam*).[9]

More than any other topic, the *Naiṣkarmya-siddhi* is concerned over the questions and conflicts arising between the way of knowledge and the way of works. With this short introduction to the problem,

[9]*Naiṣkarmyasiddhi* I.53.

we are ready to investigate the presuppositions and subsequent consequences pertaining thereto.

The first systematic work on Mīmāṃsā was the *Pūrvamīmāṃsāsūtra* of Jaimini (c. 400 B.C.). The earliest extant commentary upon this work is the *Bhāṣya* by Śabara (c. 200 A.D.). Śabara's commentary was then interpreted by two great scholars, Prabhākara (c. 650 A.D.) and Kumārila Bhaṭṭa (c. 700 A.D.). Since there are differences of interpretation between these two scholars, two sub-schools came into existence named after them: the Prabhākara school and the Bhaṭṭa school. Both of these schools maintain that action is the means to liberation - though they differ regarding the question as to whether there is such a thing as knowledge of the Self (*samyag-jñāna*). In Chapter One, verses 9-13 present the Bhaṭṭa view and verses 14-21 present the Prabhākara view.

II.ii. BHATTA MĪMĀṂSĀ

A distinctive feature of Indian philosophy is the manner in which each school conducts a systematic exposition of its own doctrine. The method of exposition adopted by each philosopher is to establish his own position through a progressive criticism of the rival views. These rival views are called the *'pūrva pakṣa'*. They are examined in sequence, beginning with the least acceptable view, followed by each subsequent view being criticized in light of the prior objection. Finally, when even the most proximate view is rejected, the philosopher's own standpoint or settled conclusion (*siddhānta*) is established. Thus, in every Indian philosophical classic whose aim is to show through dialectics that the philosophical positions that oppose Advaita are not tenable, there is a dialectical movement towards the author's final position through a progressive criticism of other perspectives.

Sureśvara states the rival (Bhaṭṭa) position as a *prima facie* view (*pūrva pakṣa*). "Since liberation arises through ritualistic action (alone), what is the use of knowledge?"[10] This is a reference to the Bhaṭṭa position (see *Śloka Vārtika, sambandhaksepa parihara* section, verses 103-110).) Kumārila admits that there is such a thing as Self-knowledge, but he denies that it has any part in the direct means to liberation. In reference to the *śruti* statement, 'the Self is to be seen',[11] he concedes that this passage points to a knowledge of the Self. However, he argues that even here, the true purport is an injunction to perform rituals. Quite implausibly, Kumārila states that it is only if and when an individual knows that his or her Self is a distinct individual soul, separate from the body and immortal, that that individual will engage in ritualistic actions for the sake of liberation.

According to Kumārila, liberation is obtained by actions alone. Four our purposes here, actions may be divided into four types: self-interested (*kāmya*),

---

[10]Ibid., I.9.

[11]*Bṛhadāraṇyaka Upaniṣad* II.iv.5.

prohibited (*nisiddha*), daily (*nitya*), and occasional (*naimittika*).[12]

Self-interested actions are desire-prompted. They are always accompanied by a specific type of fruit (*phala*) which will manifest itself at some time in a future incarnation. The *Veda* states which type of self-interested action produces what particular fruit, e.g., 'let him who desires heaven perform the *jyotiṣṭoma'*. All such actions are performed for the fulfillment of some desire so that the performer thereof may enjoy the fruits of that action. Such self-interested actions, along with all prohibited actions, i.e., murder, etc., must be given up.

Kumārila states that an individual must perform the obligatory (*nitya* and *naimittika*) rites. According to an individual's position in life, certain obligatory Vedic duties must be performed, e.g., the daily prayer as well as certain occasional duties, e.g., the birth ceremony at the birth of a son. Not only will their performance destroy the demerit contracted by previous sins, but will also avoid accruing a sin of omittance. Since the *Veda* has enjoined such actions as obligatory, their non-performance would produce new demerit. Prabhākara, on the other hand,

---

[12]See *Mīmāṃsā Paribhāṣā*, p. 43ff. The traditional distinction divides action into two types: obligatory (*nitya/naimittika*) and non-obligatory (*kāmya*). The former are commands which must be performed (categorical imperatives), either daily or on certain occasions, while the latter are injunctions which prescribe optional (hypothetical imperatives) rites. The performance of the obligatory rites does not lead to merit, but their non-performance results in demerit. If the optional rites are not performed, no demerit accrues, but if they are performed, merit accrues.

maintains that the performance of obligatory, their non-performance would produce new demerit. Prabhākara, on the other hand, maintains that the performance of obligatory rites produces no positive effects and must be performed merely to avoid the sin of omittance.

Kumārila's position is that if an individual does not perform *kāmya* and *nisiddha* actions - thereby avoiding going to either heaven or hell, and performs the daily and occasional prescribed rituals - thereby avoiding new *karma*, one obtains liberation.[13]

At this juncture, the Advaitin raises a minor objection. The present bodily existence is due to desire-prompted actions which were performed earlier. Isn't it enough for an individual to abstain from *kāmya* and *nisiddha karmas*? Why must one perform *nitya/naimittika karmas* also? In other words the question is: 'Why does the (Bhaṭṭa) Mīmāṃsaka say that the non-performance is a negative (*abhāva*) action. How can demerit arise from something negative? In other words, how can a positive something (demerit) arise from a negative something (non-performance)?

The Bhaṭṭa answer is found in their acceptance of non-cognition (*anupalabdhi*) as a valid means of knowledge (*pramāṇa*).[14] *Anupalabdhi* is the *pramāṇa* for non-existence. Just as the existence of a thing is known through the other *pramāṇas*, perception, etc.,

---

[13]*Naiṣkarmyasiddhi* I.10.

[14]*Mīmāṃsāsūtra* I.1.5. The Prabhākara School does not accept non-cognition as a valid means of knowledge.

the non-existence of a thing is known through non-cognition. Even as non-cognition cannot account for the cognition of positive entities, so too, the positive *pramāṇas* cannot serve as the means for cognizing negative facts. Since you too (the Advaitin) accept non-cognition as a *pramāṇa*, this should be obvious and unquestionable.

On the next point both Mīmāṃsa and Advaita are also in agreement. The present bodily existence is due to *karma*-in-action (*prārabdha karma*). As well, both schools agree that this stock of merit and demerit which has been set in motion in this present body can only be removed or exhausted by experience.

II.iii. PRABHĀKARA MĪMĀṂSĀ

Prabhākara and his followers hold that there is no such thing as knowledge of the Self because there is no valid means of knowledge (*pramāṇa*) to establish it.[15] As well, it is nowhere stated in the Scripture that such a knowledge exists. The only authority that they accept is the Scripture and nowhere does Scripture say anything about *'ātma-jñāna'* as a means of release. These texts stress again and again, without being able to emphasize enough, that the only means to liberation is through action.

The Advaitin raises another minor objection here. The Mīmāṃsakas presume that the Self

---

[15]*Naiṣkarmyasiddhi* I.14 *sambandhokti: tat-pratipādaka-pramāṇābhāvāt.*

(*Ātman*) is revealed or made known by a valid means of knowledge (*pramāṇa*). But, according to Advaita, this is not so. The Self is not revealed by *śruti*. The Self is self-luminous (*sva-prakāśa*) and self-established (*pra-siddha*). The work of the valid means of knowledge called Scripture (verbal testimony) is to remove all the false notions which have been superimposed upon the Self. Its work is purely negative.

Secondly, all the *pramāṇas* function only due to the presence of the Self or Consciousness. The Advaitin points out the even though all knowledge of the myriad things of the world comes through some means of valid knowledge, a means functions as a means only through the help of Consciousness. This Consciousness is presupposed in every act of knowing and it is the basis of all knowledge. It is only indirectly that all objects are established through a valid means of knowledge. They are established directly through Consciousness. And Consciousness is self-established. "Everything shines only after that shining light."[16] Even as a light is needed to reveal objects in a dark room, but no further light is necessary to reveal the light itself, so too, is Consciousness self-luminous and self-established. Thus, though all the *pramāṇas* are dependent upon Consciousness, Consciousness is not dependent upon any *pramāṇa*.

Finally, it is merit and demerit, righteousness and unrighteousness (*dharma* and *adharma*) which are known through the Scripture. The Self is both

---

[16] *Kaṭha Upaniṣad* II.2.15.

self-luminous and not an object of valid knowledge (*aprameya*).

The Mīmāṃsaka claims that the Scripture enjoins actions by means of injunctions (*vidhi*) and that such actions produce liberation. Yet, at the same time, the Mīmāṃsaka levels a charge of criticism against knowledge because there are not to be found any injunctions within Scripture which pertain to the view that knowledge gives liberation. Such a criticism is unfounded because, according to the Mīmāṃsaka themselves, injunctions pertain to the unseen fruits (*adṛṣṭa phala*) which are obtained from actions (*karma*). Knowledge, on the other hand, is said to give only seen fruits (*dṛṣṭa phala*). Thus, why should the Mīmāṃsaka raise the question about the relation between injunctions and knowledge at all?

The Prabhākara school offers three types of arguments to establish the conclusion that the Scripture enjoins action and that it is action which gives liberation. These three types of arguments are: 1) by means of reasoning (*yukti*), 2) by citing the authority of one who knows (*āpta-vākya*), and 3) by citing Scripture (*śruti*).

II.iv. ARGUMENT BY REASONING

By means of reasoning, the Prabhākara Mīmāṃsakas say that *śrutis* and *smṛtis* enjoin only action (*karma*) as their central teaching. Having searched high and low, they can find no injunction anywhere which enjoins knowledge as a means to liberation.

II.iv.1. OBJECTION

The Advaitin raises an objection: What about the *śruti* text, 'the Self is to be seen'? The Prabhākara answer is that this particular text refers to the Self as an agent and not as you (the Advaitin) perceive the Self. As was noted earlier, Mīmāṃsā considers the Self as a separate individual soul who must engage in ritualistic action in order to achieve liberation. Thus, this passage is really an injunction commanding the Self to perform rituals.

If the Advaitin claims that the Mīmāṃsaka cannot understand this text properly, perhaps the Advaitin can point out which (as yet undiscovered) pramana renders it meaningful from the perspective of knowledge. For, according to the Mīmāṃsaka, one cannot meaningfully pursue an activity which does not have the sanction of Scripture or a valid means of knowledge. Any such effort would be futile and could not possibly give the result of liberation.

Advaita, on the other hand, claims that no injunction is needed in order to remove ignorance which is the cause of bondage. The removal of ignorance requires only knowledge - even as the removal of darkness requires only light. However, the Mīmāṃsakas disagree with this position. They claim that the Advaitin proceeds on a certain presupposition. Advaitins (wrongly) believe that liberation is a mere removal or destruction of ignorance (*avidyā-naśa*). They hold that where knowledge is, ignorance is not - and that this is precisely the definition of liberation. The Mīmāṃsakas do not agree to this definition and staunchly maintain that liberation is to be achieved only through actions.

The Advaitins maintain that liberation is possible even during one's present bodily existence (*jīvanmukti*).[17] The liberated-while-living individual is in the world, though not of the world. The continuance of the body is in no way incompatible with the status of liberation. Liberation is but a change in perspective. Before release, one took the world of which the body is a part to be real; after gaining liberation one realizes that the world is an illusory appearance. If the body were real, then liberation could come only after the destruction of the body. But, since the body is not real, its continued appearance of disappearance is of no consequence. From the standpoint of the *jīvanmukta*, there is no body at all.

On the other hand, the Mīmāṃsakas say that liberation is possible only in an unembodied state.

---

[17]*Bṛhadāraṇyaka Upaniṣad* IV.4.7.

Both schools actually maintain that liberation means 'there is no association with a body' (*aśarīratva*). They differ in that, while Advaita interprets this statement figuratively, Mīmāṃsā interprets it literally.

Thus, to employ terminology which we just used in another context, Advaita says that liberation can be a seen fruit while Mīmāṃsā defines liberation as an unseen fruit.

II.v. ARGUMENT BY AUTHORITY

To support their argument-by-reasoning, the Mīmāṃsakas next proceed to substantiate their doctrine of action by claiming that Jaimini is a knower of the *Veda's* inner truth. At the very least, his word is an accepted authority (*āpta vākya*). Since he was an acknowledge authority on Vedic matters, when he said "since the ultimate purport of the *Veda* is to enjoin actions, the passages not enjoining actions are (in themselves) purportless".[18]

One traditional division of the *Veda* is into: injunctive statements (*vidhi vākya)* and existential statements (*siddhārtha vākya*). According to Mīmāṃsā, an existential statement is meaningful and valid only when it is made subsidiary to an injunctive statement. An existential statement must be construed along with an injunction. The former is of secondary importance and the latter is

[18]*Mīmāṃsāsūtra* I.2.1.

of primary importance - with the latter giving meaning to the former.

As we have already noted, the Mīmāṃsakas contend that since existential statements convey what is already known through other sources of knowledge, they are merely a restatement (*anuvāda*) and dependent upon what they convey. Thus, in actuality, they are not a source of knowledge at all.

For instance, when the text 'mediate on the Self' is considered the injunctive statement, the question arises, 'what is the Self?' Thus, the existential statement '(the Self is) *satyam, jñānam, anantam*', clarifies and gives information to the injunctive statement. The existential statement gains validity and meaningfulness by its act of clarifying the injunctive statement.

On the other hand, injunctive statements do not encounter such difficulties. What they convey (enjoining an action) cannot be known through any other source of knowledge. Not only are they independent in respect of what they convey, but they are also unique as a particular source of knowledge. For instance, the text which enjoins the performance of the offering in the fire (*Agnihotra*) conveys what cannot otherwise be known.

II.v.1. OBJECTION

The Advaitins raise an objection here. The argument that injunctive statements are primary and existential statements are mere restatements, secondary, and gain meaning only from injunctive statements cannot be accepted. Does a sentence become a restatement when what it conveys is already given by some other valid means of knowledge? Or, does it become a restatement just because it states something existent?

Obviously the Advaitin will accept the claim that a sentence is merely a restatement if it is not original and independent of what it conveys. But they object to the claim that a sentence becomes a restatement simply because it intimates an existent object - especially when what it conveys is entirely new and independent of any other means of valid knowledge.

The *Veda* is held to be impersonal (*apauruṣeya*). Thus Vedic sentences convey, whether they are assertive or injunctive, information which is new and cannot be conveyed by any other means. The *Upaniṣads* convey knowledge of the trans-empirical, ever-existent *Brahman*. This knowlege is impersonal and independent of any other means of knowledge. Thus, it must be accorded validity, even as existential statements independent of injunctive statements.

II.vi. ARGUMENT BY SCRIPTURE

This argument takes two aspects: that which relates to the 'form' (Grammar) of Scripture and that which relates to the 'content' (Text) of Scripture. Regarding the actual text, the Mīmāṃsaka invokes the *Īśa Upaniṣad* passage: "Let an individual desire to live a hundred years here on Earth ever performing ritual works".[19] The Mīmāṃsaka interprets this verse to mean that the purport of the *Veda* is to enjoin actions.

II.vi.1. OBJECTION

Advaita objects to the Mīmāṃsaka interpretation of this *Īśa Upaniṣad* passage in three ways: Regarding agency, enjoyership, and eligibility. Per the former, according to Advaita, the Self (*Ātman*) is neither an agent nor an enjoyer. To support this aspect of their objection, the Advaitin asks, 'Is 'x' (Jaimini) the body, or is he the Self'? If he is the Self, then, according to the Scripture, the Self is not an agent (*karta*). This would have the consequences of eliminating 'x' as the agent who performs actions and lives for 100 years.[20] On the other hand, if 'x' is the body, then, according to Jaimini, the results of performed actions are to be achieved in a life yet to come. Therefore, if one is the body and the body is perishable (which is accepted by everyone), then it follows that this present body will never enjoy the fruits of one's actions. There is no third entity left to enjoy the fruits of one's actions. The Self may survive death, but it is not an agent of action. The body may be an agent of action, but it does not survive death.[21]

---

[19] *Īśa Upaniṣad* 2. *kurvann eveha karmāṇi jijīviṣet śataṁ samāḥ.*

[20] See *Muṇḍaka Upaniṣad* III.1.1. - Two birds, ever united companions, cling to the self-same tree. of these two, one eats the sweet berry. The other looks on without eating. Also see *Bhagavadgītā.*

[21] See *Naiṣkarmyasiddhi* I.92-93.

Regarding eligibility, it does not arise in regards to the Self, but in regards to the body. According to Advaita, the Self is pure, one, and non-dual. It is not revealed by any *pramāṇa*. It is the non-self which is revealed by valid means of knowledge. In practical life, the Self is confused with, and attempted to be known, through the adjuncts of the body. But it is the non-self, specifically the body, which is composed of adjuncts or parts. The Self is other than the non-self, even as the non-self is other than the Self. The question Sureśvara asks is, 'which part of you is eligible - the body, the mind, or the Self?'.

Finally, the Self is not an enjoyer (*bhokta*). The body, along with adjuncts, is needed for pleasure and pain to be experienced. Yet, the body, its adjuncts like the mind, etc., and experience are all external and objective while the Self is internal. There is no connection between the body which is subject to pleasure and pain and the Self which is not. The Self is not affected by the mind. Thus it makes even less sense to say that the Self is affected by the senses, the body, or external objects, which are progressively farther away. Therefore, the Self cannot be said to be an enjoyer and external things cannot be said to affect the Self.[22]

II.vii. NATURE OF SCRIPTURE

According to Prabhākara, knowledge of the Self cannot arise because the Advaitin seeks such knowledge in scriptural statements (*śruti vākya*), and the central element of the Scripture is verbs (which signify action).[23] The Mīmāṃsaka seeks to justify this position by a theory of learning according to which the meanings of words are claimed to be learnt only in the context of actions. For instance, children observe the actions which take place around them and relate these actions to verbal commands which accompany them, i.e., the father says, 'bring the cow'. By a process of insertion and elimination, the children come to understand the meanings of the words 'bring', 'cow', etc. Their claim is that it is only in such action-oriented command situations that words become meaningful.

Taking this as one's example, it is easy to see from where the Mīmāṃsaka has come to claim that assertive statements are auxiliary to injunctive statements. It is only in injunctive statements that the verb is the principal part of speech. The other parts of speech such as nouns, adjectives, etc., have to be understood only as modifying the verb. And furthermore, the injunctive suffix within the verb is the most important factor. For, the injunctive suffix signifies what is technically called 'what-is-to-

---

[23]Ibid., I.19.

be-done' or the *niyoga*. Action, especially right action, is at the heart of their system.

Extending the consequences of such a claim, if it is the case that secular words have action (*niyoga*) as their purport, it must go without saying that the *Veda* has *niyoga* as its sole purport also. Why does this follow? Secular objects are known through empirical means of knowledge (*pramāṇa)*, i.e., perception, inference, etc. If the *Veda* were to give merely knowledge about the existent, it would not be an independent valid means of knowledge. Yet, it is only the *Veda* that super-normal or extra-empirical actions or *niyoga* are known. It is for this reason that *niyoga* or right spiritual action is described by the Mīmāṃsakas as that which is novel and not known through any other valid means of knowledge except *Veda* (or *śabda*).

Therefore, the Mīmāṃsakas declare that what the *Veda* teaches is primarily action. It is not individual desire which prompts action - but the cognition of a command or *niyoga*. For instance, a servant executes an act, i.e., cooking dinner, because his/her master commands him or her to do so - even though the servant may not have any desire to do so of its own volition. Likewise, the *Veda*, which is the supreme master, issues certain commands. Humanity's wisdom lies in obeying these commands. The Vedic *niyoga* is impervious.[24] In short, the *Veda* is a *niyoga-śāstra* - a text which teaches what-is-to-be-done. Any text which does not

---

[24]*Mīmāṃsāsūtra* I.2.1. *āmnāyasya kriyārthatvāt ānarthakyam atadarthānām.*

prescribe either a positive imperative or a negative prohibition is meaningless, according to the Mīmāṃsakas.[25] For instance, the text: "He cried", states that *Agni* cried in anguish and his tears turned to silver. This is just a descriptive statement of what happened. As such, it is a *siddha-vākya*. Thus, if taken in isolation, such a statement has no meaning. The 'why' behind this statement is that there is a prohibition behind offering silver as a gift in a sacrifice. The reason is that 'when *Agni* cried, his tears turned to silver'. In this way, the descriptive narration of *Agni's* crying gains meaning by being related syntactically to the prescriptive text prohibiting silver in a sacrifice. The same logic holds good for the statement 'meditate upon the Self' (*Ātma ityeva upausita*). According to the Mīmāṃsakas, this statement is meaningful only as a prescription to perform the act of meditation.

II.vii.1. OBJECTION

Śaṅkara refuted the Mīmāṃsaka claim that the verb (which denotes action) alone gives meaning to the words of a sentence[26] The basic position of Advaita claims that the purport of the Scripture is to state the knowledge/fact of the ever-existent

---

[25]The Bhāṭṭa view holds that the motive for obeying Vedic commands stems from an individual's desire to acquire pleasure and avoid pain. The Prabhākara view believes that the *Veda* is not dependent upon the human will. Both schools believe there is a necessity for obeying the commands of the *Veda* however.

[26]*Brahmasūtrabhāṣya*, I.1.4.

Brahman. Words cannot fail to reveal their meanings no matter to what purpose they are being employed. Descriptive statements convey knowledge and as knowledge they remove ignorance. Thus, it is gratuitious to declare that knowledge of an established fact is meaningless. For instance, the knowledge that what was mistaken for a snake is only a rope, puts an end to an individual's fear - and this is definitely a purportful result.

The Mīmāṃsakas claimed that any sentence which did not have its purport in action was a mere statement of something which could be known by one of the other valid means of knowledge, e.g., perception, etc. But, there is no valid reason or established law which declares that an established entity must be perceived through perception. Certainly perceptibility is not the only criterion for an established fact to be know. An established fact may be imperceptible or unknowable (by perception) due to its being either extremely subtle or lacking in distinguishing marks, i.e., protons or righteousness.

As well, an established entity may be imperceptible in differing senses. *Brahman* is said to be imperceptible and realizable only in experience. Righteousness (*dharma*) is imperceptible while being the result of an act. *Dharma* is known only from the Scripture while *Brahman* is ultimately unknowable. To know *Brahman* is to be *Brahman*. Knowlege of righteousness, leads to meaningful acts. But even knowledge of *Brahman*, though not an act, is meaningful in that it removes ignorance.

Further, there are ample Vedic texts which do have the purport of teaching *Brahman*[27] in contradistinction to the Mīmāṃsaka claim to the contrary. By the application of the six criteria of meaning[28], the purport or intended meaning of certain statements can well be determined that *Brahman* is the content of the teaching of these Upaniṣadic texts. These six criteria are fundamental to Mīmāṃsaka thought and it would be farfetched, indeed, to even try to employ them in interpreting these texts as exhorting action. There is an explicit reference to *Brahman* in these texts and one should not unwarrantedly understand any other meaning by twisting the texts unnecessarily.

The six characteristic marks (*ṣaḍliṅga*) are: the harmony of the initial and concluding passages (*upakrama-upasaṁhāra*), repetition (*abhyāsa*), novelty (*apūrvatā*), fruitfulness (*phala*), glorification by eulogistic passages or condemnation by deprecatory passages (*arthavāda*), and intelligibility in the light of reasoning (*upapatti*).

For example, to show that the non-dual *Brahman* is the central teaching of the *Upaniṣads*, Advaita aplies these six criteria to a passage in the sixth chapter of the *Chāndogya Upaniṣad*. The text opens with the words, "As Being alone, O dear One, was this in the beginning, one only, without a second." The chapter ends with the words, "All this is of the

---

27See *Chāndogya Upaniṣad* VI.2.1; *Aitareya Upaniṣad* II.1.1.1; *Bṛhadāraṇyaka Upaniṣad* II.5.19; *Muṇḍaka Upaniṣad* II.2.11.

28See the introduction to the *Bhāmatī*: *upakrama 'pasaṁhārāv abhyāso, 'pūrvatā phalam arthavādo 'papattī ca liṅgaṁ tātparya nirṇaye.*

essence of it." Thereby is established that there is harmony between the beginning and concluding passages. Within this chapter the statement 'that thou art' (*tat tvam asi*) is repeated nine times. That the truth is the One, non-dual *Brahman* (which is the subject taught in this chapter) cannot be obtained by any other means is also expounded herein. "He knows who has a preceptor; for him there is delay only so long as he is not free (from the body), and then he becomes (with *Brahman*)", speaks of the fruit or result of the knowledge of *Brahman*. The non-dual *Brahman* is glorified in such passages as, "Did you ask for that instruction by which the unheard becomes heard, the unknown becomes known, the un-understood becomes understood?" And lastly, this chapter presents for its teaching that *Brahman* is the One, non-dual Reality. For instance, "Just as by means of a single lump of clay, all things earthen are known, all transformations are verbal and therefore are only name; earth alone is real", such passages seek to establish the non-dual *Brahman* by means of analogical reasoning.

Secondly, it cannot be said that Scriptural texts solely refer to an agent of action because there exist texts which explicitly deny the possibility of agent, act, and instrument thereof. For instance, there is the text: "With what would he see what?"[29] This text repudiates all distinctions possible upon the realization of the Self.

---

[29]*Bṛhadāraṇyaka Upaniṣad* II.4.13.

Certainly it is true, recognised, and accepted by all Advaitins that *Brahman* is an established fact (*siddha vastu*). But this alone does not, nor cannot be the reason why it (*Brahman*) should be perceived by the senses or other valid means of knowledge. An established entity may or may not be perceptible to the senses. As was stated earlier, perceptibility is not the criterion for an established fact existing prior to the operation of a valid means of knowledge.

Jaimini's intention in saying that Scriptural texts not referring to any act are meaningless is only to show that the *arthavāda* or eulogistic meaning/condemnatory meaning (like the stories and myths which have no cognitive meaning in themselves) must be related to texts prescribing acts to acquire meaning. He does not refer to existential or negative statements (*siddha* and *niṣedha vākya*) which have their own meanings independently of any act.

Adherents of the Prabhākara position maintain that even if knowledge of the Self were to exist - it doesn't, but suppose they were to grant such for the sake of argument, even then it will not change the claim that action is the central purport of the Scripture. They osit that the relation between knowledge and action must be one of three types: either 1) knowledge is subsidiary to action, 2) action is subsidiary to knowledge, or 3) their relationship is on an equal footing.[30]

No matter which of the three relationships is chosen, release must come through some form of

---

[30] *Naiṣkarmyasiddhi* I.20.

action. Knowledge alone, and by itself, is refuted. Knowledge can be found only in conjunction with action in one of these three types of relationships. This being so, whether one accepts that spiritual knowledge exists or not, in any case it cannot, of itself, lead to liberation. For every station of life (*āśrama*), according to each individual's capacity, it is action which brings release. It is action through speech (study the *Veda* and speak the truth); it is action through the mind (make the mind pure and tranquil); and it is action through the body (perform the daily and ocasional duties) - *karma* through *vāk*, *manas*, and *kāya* brings release and nothing else.

II.viii. ADVAITA VEDĀNTA'S REBUTTAL

According to Advaita, action (*karma*) cannot give liberation *(mokṣa)*. This is due to the fact that the effects of action are of four types and liberation does not fall into any of its four categories.[31] The effects of an action pertain to either: origination (*utpattiḥ*), attainment (*āpti)*, modification (*vikṛti*), or purification (*saṁskṛti*). However, according to advaita, liberation is but the destruction of ignorance (*avidyā nāśa*). We will go deeper into this later on, but for now let it suffice to note that action cannot remove ignorance (and thereby give liberation) simply because: liberation is not something which is pro-

[31]Ibid. I.23. These are listed in I.53; in *Upadeśa Sāhasrī* XVII.50; and in the *Dakṣiṇāmūrti* hymn with Sureśvara's *Mānasollāsa Commentary*.

duced - liberation is ever-existent (*nitya*); liberation is not something to be attained - it is already attained; liberation is not something to be modified - since the Self (*Ātman*) is unchangeable (*avikāri*) and immutable (*kūṭastha*); and liberation is not purification - the Self is eternally pure. Action is itself an effect of ignorance and hence could never destroy it. Action and ignorance are not incompatible in regards to eithe their source, nature, effect, or field of operation.

Action cannot give liberation because liberation is nothing more than remaining in one's own state (*svarūpa sthiti*). It is only knowledge which can remove ignorance even as light is the only remedy for darkness. Even as darkness cannot remove darkness, so too, action cannot remove ignorance. Action is dependent upon superimposition (*adhyāsa*) and superimposition is dependent upon ignorance. Thus, every action is due to ignorance.

If this were not damaging enough, the Advaitin continues by saying that even if it were granted (for the sake of argumentation) that liberation could be achieved through action, still insurmountable problems would exist. The question can be posed, 'Is liberation the effect of one action or of all actions combined'?

If liberation is the effect of one single action, then all other actions are useless. If there is one single action which confers liberation as its fruit, then all other actions would be rendered superfluous and useless. This would have the effect of rendering almost every single Vedic injunction as prohibited (*pratisiddha*) since they would involve uselessness.

Advaita's view is not open to this criticism since it maintains that liberation comes through the destruction of ignorance and all Vedic injunctions have their validity only within the realm of ignorance before liberation arises.

If liberation is the effect of all actions combined, then they, in combination, are the equivalent of one single action and this goes contrary to the Mīmāṃsaka theory that actions are of various kinds. Mīmāṃsā claims that every kind of ritualistic action, without exception, has its own specific result. Yet, how can every action give but a single result? Neither is it possible for a single individual to perform all the myriad actions which go with all the different stations of life (*āśramas*). And if all the actions of one particular *āśrama* produce liberation, then since in the cause there is a special excellence, there must also be a special excellence in liberation. However, there are no gradations in liberation.

According to the Mīmāṃsaka, specific actions have specific fruits. Yet, there are no Vedic injunctions which delineate what particular action gives liberation. The declared purpose of ritualistic actions is to consume the effects of an individual's previous sins. So, which action gives liberation? Daily (*nitya*) and occasional (*naimittika*) actons remove sins; self-interested (*kāmya*) actions give enjoyment; prohibited (*pratisiddha*) actions give sin. There are no other types of actions. Thus, nowhere does the Vedic orpus state that action gives liberation.

As well, the *śruti* itself does not say that action gives liberation. According to Advaita, liberation is trans-empirical. The job of the Scripture is merely to suggest the means-end relation. Its role is purely informative. The knowledge which Scripture gives, like all knowledge, is declared to be controlled by an already existent reality.[32] As such it is revelatory and its function is merely to reveal the nature of a thing.

If an individual is desirous of heaven, then an appropriate action must be performed. Scripture's work is to state this means-end relation. 'Do you want heaven?' - 'Then perform this *yajña*'. Scripture does not, nor cannot, compel an individual to perform any action. All it can do is to inform what steps to take if a desire is present. It is the desire that leads to action and not the information itself. One may perform an action, not perform that action, or perform that action differently according to one's individual whim - but, in regards to a fact there is nothing to be done. As Maṇḍana said, 'Scripture gives one knowledge of the means to a particular desire' (*iṣṭa-sādhanatā-jñāna*).

In concluding this particular rebuttal, Sureśvara makes a subtle dig at the Mīmāṃsakas. He alludes to a well-known story about an Indian mother-in-law and her daughter-in-law. The mother-in-law had overheard her daughter-in-law telling a beggar to leave the premises because "Go away, we've nothing for you here". Infuriated at her daughter-in-law, the mother-in-law shouts, "What right have you to tell beggars that we have nothing here?" Then the mother-in-law turns around and

---

[32]See *Bṛhadāraṇyaka Upaniṣad* IV.5.15 and I.4.10.

yells at the beggar saying, "Go away, we've nothing for you here".

Sureśvara is saying, 'your words are really our words' and 'you believe what we believe'. Since both Advaita and Mīmāṃsā uphold the avoidance of prohibited and self-interested actions, as well as the fact that obligatory daily and occasional rituals do not produce any positive results, our doctrines really do not differ. Thus it follows, even on the Mīmāṃsaka's own principles, that liberation is not to be achieved through action.

II.ix. ADVAITA VEDĀNTA'S THESIS

After having refuted the Mīmāṃsaka view that liberation arises through action, Sureśvara now advances several arguments to support his contention that liberation is but the cessation of ignorance (which arises only through knowledge of the Self).

Within the empirical world it is usually the case that an individual performs an action, or abstains from performing an action, according to that individual's own personal desire or aversion. These desires and aversions are determined by empirical sources of knowledge. But the problem which arises concerning liberation is not empirical (*dṛṣṭa-phala*) but trans-empirical (*adṛṣṭa-phala*). The individual desires liberation. The Mīmāṃsaka claim is that action is the means to liberation. But will a self-interested action, which is to give unseen future fruits (liberation), proceed and succeed along the same empirical lines?

If this action is based upon authoritative right knowledge (*pramāṇa mūlaka*), either secular or Scriptural, then Mīmāṃsā is correct. On the other hand, if this action is based upon a wrong knowledge (*mithyā jñāna*) and renunciation of action is correct, then Advaita's view is the right one. In other words, does all prompting to action arise from ignorance or is action the correct means to fulfillment, no matter what the end?

Sureśvara says that '*śruti* reveals like the sun reveals'. Even as the sun shines alike on the good and bad revealing both, so too, Scripture is value-free, commitment-free, neutral, revealing merely the means-end relation. Individuals' desire what is pleasurable and dislike what is painful. Scripture tells what the means to the good are and how to avoid the bad. It does not confer any power on anything whatsoever. Desire and aversion are natural to individuals and are not something given by Scripture.

An individual's personal conception of good and bad, of desire and aversion arises from ignorance. People act due to wrong knowledge (*mithyā-jñāna*). They give value to things due to this ignorance. Being confused about what is really good (the Self), individuals resort to all types of desire and aversion in an attempt to obtain liberation. The Scripture is most helpful in this endeavour because liberation is a sphere which no other means of knowledge has access to.

That the Self is never separate from the 'good', the 'pleasant', the 'blissful' can be demonstrated through perception, inference, and revelation.

Perceptual experience exists in the state of deep-sleep. From the non-existence of pain and misery in the sleep state one can conclude that one is in a state of happiness or bliss. As the Scripture says, "Crossing the bund of the experience of waking and dream, the *puruṣa,* though blind, becomes who who is not blind, though wounded, becomes one who is not wounded, though suffering from disease, becomes one who is not suffering from disease."[33] This happiness is in the Self is directly experienced and not inferred. And because in sleep, this state of happiness is experienced, it testifies to the nature of the Self.

That the Self is blissful can also be demonstrated through inference. Every individual wants happiness. There is the evidence of everyone's individual experience who say after waking up from sleep: 'Happily did I sleep; I knew nothing when I was asleep'. This reflective cognition of happiness is grounded in the experience of sleep - for without the latter the former would not be possible. Nor may it be said that since in sleep there are no recognized means of knowledge there can be no experience of happiness or lack of misery. Such experiences require no instrument of knowledge for they are self-luminous and self-revealed (thereby requiring no external channel of cognition). Everyone seeks the Self because it is the source of happiness, nay, it is happiness itself.

---

[33]*Chāndogya Upaniṣad* VIII.iv.2.

Thirdly, there is the Scriptural authority which declares *'ānandam brahman'* - the Self is bliss.[34] There are other texts like: "From bliss, indeed, all creatures come into being; in bliss they live; and unto bliss they return. Hence bliss is *Brahman*."[35] The nearer a thing is to the self, the dearer it is. Those who do not realize this fundamental fact and consider things other than the self to be dearer meet with disappointment and disillusionment. Thus, the Self is the real good. One should not give ultimate value to the things of the world, 'this vale of tears'. If one acts due to wrong knowledge, misery will be the result.

What Scripture does is merely to inform one of this fact. It has no ability to confer power on anything. It does not create the power in fire to burn; nor does it create agency or enjoyership in the Self; nor does it create the attainability of heaven or some other 'desirable' thing; nor does it create the instrumental nature of a sacrifice.

Thus, after demonstrating that an individual who does not know the Self cannot attain the Self through the performance of Vedic injunctions and prohibitions, Sureśvara now goes on to show wthat no action çan possibly acquire the Self because it is already self-attained. The Scripture's real purpose is to state the appropriate means for the attainment of the Self, as well as what to avoid.

Attainment may be said to be of two types and avoidance is likewise two-fold. There is the attain-

---

34 *Bṛhadāraṇyaka Upaniṣad* III.ix.28.
35 *Taittirīya Upaniṣad* III.6.

ment of the unattained through ignorance and there is attainment of what is really to be attained. Likewise, there is the avoidance of the avoided of its own accord, and there is the avoidance of what is really to be avoided. The first type in each case is not attainment or avoidance in the real sense of the term. Something is already attained, or avoided, but through ignorance one thinks that it is no so, i.e., discovering the gold necklance around one's neck which was thought lost, or, avoiding a demon which turns out to be but a shadow. The real sense of attainment or avoidance occurs when one attains what was not previously attained, i.e., a wealth which was not previously possessed or avoids what needs to be avoided, i.e., a snake which is really present.

These examples have been given by Sureśvara in order to demonstrate that the Scripture gives information regarding things which exist empirically. The sruti tells the appropriate means to attain what is good and to avoid what is evil. But, and this is extremely important, the other two cases stand 'attained' or 'avoided' by their very nature.

Thus, liberation or enlightenment is but the dispelling of the illusion that there is something to be newly attained or avoided. Action cannot give this liberating knowledge. It is not action, but knowledge which dispells ignorance. Ignorance is the only obstacle to attaining the 'lost' necklace or of avoiding the demon. One obtains the objects of the world through action, but the Self is 'attainable' solely through knowledge. Since ego-hood or *jīva-bhāva* doesn't really exist, it is already avoided. The Self eternally is, and thus is already attained. It is through ignorance that one does not realize this. It is through knowledge that one attains the already attained (*prāptasya prāptiḥ*).

Now, since action itself arises from ignorance, it cannot remove or destroy ignorance. But knowledge is the opposite of ignorance, even as light is the opposite of darkness, and thus knowledge removes ignorance even as the sun removes darkness.[36]

Sureśvara anticipates a possible objection here. The Mīmāṃsaka may say that it is true that liberation is not in a state of bondage. However, individuals, Scripture, teacher, and all the other effects of ignorance are (physically) in a state of bondage and therefore liberation is something to be attained in the real-sense-of-the-term. And if this is the case, then this attainment must be obtained through action.

Sureśvara answers, 'no', because right-knowledge is based on the self-revealed *Brahman* alone. Right knowledge depends upon Scripture only for its arisal, but once risen, it does not depend on the Scripture for its removal of ignorance. Yet, as we observed earlier, action depends upon ignorance both for its rise and for the production of its effects after it has risen.

The Mīmāṃsaka claims that knowledge of the Self also arises from ignorance, even as action arises from ignorance, because it, too, presupposes differ-

---

[36]*Naiṣkarmyasiddhi* I.35. *karmājñāna-samutthatvān nālaṁ mohāpanuttaye samyag-jñānaṁ virodhy asya tāmisrasyāṁśumān iva.*

ence (Scripture, teacher, pupil, etc.). And if this is so, then it also is not competent to remove ignorance.

Not so, replies Sureśvara, because even though we admit that duality is present before this knowledge arises, once the knowledge of the Self does arise, duality disappears. Right knowledge makes a distinction only for its origination. But once it has arisen, right knowledge needs nothing else to perform its work and its results arise immediately.

A second objection is then raised: We both acknowledge that wrong knowledge exists and due to its presence an individual pursues empirical things. It is your (Sureśvara's) contention that right knowledge is needed to overcome wrong knowledge. But why do you claim that wrong knowledge cannot (also) be removed by action? In order for an individual to know that a demon is but a shadow, all that one need to is to move closer and thereby perceive that the 'demon' is but a shadow.

The Advaitin replies that it is not the act of moving closer which is the remover of the shadow-demon ignorance, but knowledge of the substratum (*adhiṣṭhāna*). Once the substratum of the error, or the shadow itself, is known, the ignorance vanishes. The act of moving closer certainly may help in obtaining this knowledge, but it is the knowledge itself which is the remover of the ignorance - and not an action alone.

The Mīmāṃsaka raises a third objection.[37] As far as we can see, even according to Advaita,

---

[37]Ibid., I,35.

knowledge of the Self must arise only from ignorance. How is that? Because one must presuppose difference, i.e., the knower, the known, and the act of knowledge must all be different. Yet, according to Advaita, the claim is put forth that anything which arises from ignorance is not competent to remove ignorance.

The Advaitin replies, it is certainly true that it would appear that in order for knowledge of the Self to arise, there must be a distinction between the teacher, the student, and what is taught. Such a duality we do admit (even though it is ontologically unreal) - until the knowledge of the Self arises. However, note that once knowledge of the Self arises, duality disappears. Right knowledge, only for its origination by an ignorant individual, seems to make a distinction. But, once right knowledge arises, it has no need of anything else (i.e., duality in any of its manifestations) to do its work. As well, once right knowledge arises, its results occur immediately.

To sum up: 1) *Ātma-jñāna* arises from *avidyā* (in a qualified sense). The content of *ātma-jñāna* is the Self (which removes all distinctions) while the content of action is the not-self (which makes distinctions).

2) *Ātma-jñāna* requires the help of ignorance only for its origination and not for doing its work. Action requires duality both for its origination as well as its work.

3) Knowledge is independent (*sva-tantra*) in doing its work, while action is always 'other-dependent' (*para-tantra*).

4) Knowledge always gives immediate results while action gives results which involve a time-lag. (Besides the fruit (*phala*) of any action - which may or not be immediate, there is a latent tendency (*saṁskāra*) which always involves duration).

II.x. ACTION INVOLVES "DOERSHIP"

The Mīmāṃsakas raised an objection that right-knowledge is sometimes contradicted by wrong-knowledge, i.e., notions of doership still raise their head.[38] The Mīmāṃsakas concede for the sake of argument that *ātma-jñāna* has arisen. Still, a doubt lingers in their minds. Individuals are observed to consider themselves as doers and enjoyers. This must mean that *mithyā-jñāna* has sublated the *ātma-jñāna*. Thus, they conclude that right knowledge can be sublated by wrong-knowledge on the basis of observed experience.

The Advaitin answers: ignorance has two aspects: non-apprehension (*agrahaṇa*) and mis-apprehension (*viparyaya*). The former is 'not knowing the truth' while the latter is 'knowing the truth otherwise'. Both aspects are products of ignorance. When ignorance is removed, mis-apprehension is removed. When the cause of mis-aprehension is removed, the effect or wrong knowledge is also removed. Thus, right knowledge is the sublator and wrong knowledge is what is sublated. Being sublated thusly, it cannot rise up again. It has been

---

[38]Ibid., I.38.

destroyed, root and branch. Logic tells us that what has been sublated cannot later rise up to be a sublator.

Sureśvara concludes that ignorance, once overcome by right knowledge, can never sublate knowledge. When right knowledge has sublated ignorance, latent tendencies (*vāsanā* or *saṁskāra*) are produced which in subsequent similar circumstances arise up to prompt the seer to remember the truth.[39]

Action involves ignorance. Without ignorance there would be no life in the world in the ordinary sense of that term. To press home his point, Sureśvara invokes the logical principles of copresence and co-absence (*anvaya-vyatireka*): Given *avidyā*, there is *saṁsāra*. Given the absence of *avidyā*, there is the absence of *saṁsāra*. Or, to state it in other terms, those individuals who possess ignorance and look upon themselves as such-and-such, a doer, enjoyer, etc., are servants to *avidyā* and all the imperious injunctions of the Scripture. Such an individual's acts sting him or her again and again by the good or bad commandments of the *Veda*.

Being tied to the terrible ocean of pain called *saṁsāra*, birth follows death and death follows birth, inexorably and inevitably. Ignorance (*avidyā*), desire (*kāma*), and action (*karma*) keep one tied to the wheel of existence. The great statements of the *śruti* are there to inform one as to the way to destroy this bondage. The *Bṛhadāraṇyaka Upaniṣad* says: "When one is released from all the desires that bind the

---

[39]Ibid.

heart, then mortals even here become immortal and realize *Brahman*."[40] Such a one is *akāma*, *niṣkāma*, *ātmakāma*, and *āptakāma*.

II.xi ACTION IS AN AID TO LIBERATION

According to Advaita, *karma* is an indirect aid to liberation. As such, action has an important place in the preparatory stages. It is said to be an indirect means (*arudupakaraka*). Sureśvara says that dispassion or renunciation (*vairāgya*) arises in the heart of an individual who has amassed much merit and has a mind which has been purified (*citta-śuddhi*) by performing *nitya-naimittika karmas*.[41]

Vairāgya, in this context, means a distaste for both heaven and hell, for this world and the next. It arises when an individual knows that the fruits of desire prompted actions are: impermanent, surpassable, and always mixed with suffering.

When dispassion has arisen in one's mind, the alluring power of passion is no longer able to entice one in exchange for a prospective pleasure. As Maṇḍana said,

> Because the Self as Consciousness is of the very nature of *Brahman*, reali-zation of *Brahman* consists in the manifestation of one's own Self that results from the rubbing away of impurities as if from a crystal.[42]

---

[40]*Bṛhadāraṇyaka Upaniṣad* IV.iv.7.
[41]*Naiṣkarmyasiddhi* I.45,47.
[42]*Brahmasiddhi* p. 121.

Thus, the mind should be made pure, clear, and tranquil so that it will naturally and spontaneously incline towards the inmost Self. The *nitya-naimittika karmas*, when routinely performed, turn the mind inwards and once their work is done, disappear of their own accord. This is their greatness - in that they purify the mind. The basis for the thesis that actions done in a pure spirit as offerings to God will drop away after purifying the mind finds its justification in the idea that the Self is naturally pure. And, once the mind is pure, actions are unnecessary.

Sureśvara quotes the *Bhagavadgītā* to support this thesis:

> The sage uses action as the means for climbing towards the heights of *yoga*. Restraint and serenity are the means for one who has attained.[43]

First one should plough the ground, then sow the seed and leave it alone to germinate.

The initial stage is a preliminary renunciation or *vividiṣā-sannyāsa*. At this level, one renounces in order to fulfill one's desire to know. It is also called *sarva-karma-sannyāsa*. This aspirant is a seeker, a *sādhaka*. Next comes the *vidvat-sannyāsa* or stage when the aspirant is a knower, a *siddha*, an accomplished one. This is renunciation after knowing the truth.

---

[43]*Bhagavadgītā* VI.3. See *Naiṣkarmyasiddhi* I.51.

Sureśvara puts all this in a nutshell: obligatory and occasional actions lead to purification/merit. Purification destroys one's demerit which leads to a pure mind. A pure mind leads to partial renunciation and renunciation leads to a desire for liberation. A desire for liberation impells one to search for a means thereto and this search enables the mind to incline towards the Self. This leads to a complete renunciation which finally bestows liberation once ignorance is destroyed.

If an individual studies the *Upaniṣads* and then declares that he hasn't obtained liberation, it is precisely because he has not gone through the preparatory stages first. Action, by itself, cannot bring about liberation - but action is an indisputable aid thereto. This is a fact which is very often overlooked in summaries and criticisms of Advaita Vedānta. There is a very definite path of spiritual exercises (*sādhana*) and it behooves an individual not to become lost in the sublties of doctrine to the detriment of realization. The time honored proces is: *śruti, yukti, anubhava*. First comes 'hearing' the doctrine. Until that is completely digested and made one's own, with all that it entails, one is not qualified or fit to enter into a critical and analytical discussion of why *mokṣa* has not occurred.

As has earlier been explained, the result of action is that something is either: produced, attained, modified, or purified.[44] *Mokṣa* has nothing to do with any of these. The Self is neither to be produced, attained, modified, or purified. Thus, action

---

[44]*Naiṣkarmyasiddhi* I.53.

can never be a direct means to it. *Mokṣa* is not in need of action's acts - though action may serve as an aid thereto.

CHAPTER THREE

III. SAMUCCAYA

III.i. INTRODUCTION

Since it has been shown that action alone cannot remove ignorance, the possibility is raised of action-cum-knowledge as the destroyer of *avidyā*.[1] Sureśvara is known as a champion of the view which maintains that liberation has nothing to do with the performance of actions. Three views are advanced regarding the joint operation of action and knowledge: Some hold that 1) knowledge is primary and action is secondary: 2) action is primary and knowledge is secondary; and 3) knowledge and action are equally important. Sureśvara refutes all of these views - whether propounded by Bhartṛprapañca, Brahmadatta, or Maṇḍana.

Jñāna-karma-samuccaya is of two kinds: sequential combination (*krama-samuccaya*) and simultaneous combination (*sama-samuccaya*). The first question the Advaitin asks an advocate of *jñāna-karma-samuccaya* is, 'which type are you advocating'? Strictly speaking, the former is no combination at all. And regarding *sama-samuccaya*, it has three possible combinations: either action is primary or knowledge is primary, or they are of equal status.

---

[1]See *Naiṣkarmyasiddhi* I.54-79.

Before considering the Mīmāṃsaka's response, let us analyze this theory of combination. According to Advaita, action can never be the means and knowledge the end product. Why? Because liberation is said to be imperishable (*nitya-phala*) while the fruits of *karma* are only perishable (*anitya-phala*). Or, again, knowledge by its very nature is *pramāṇa vastu tantra*. That is, knowledge can only be obtained through a valid means of knowledge (*pramāṇa*) and, as the object, so the knowledge. As we said earlier, knowledge is object-dependent. But, action (*karma* or *upāsana*) is *puruṣa tantra*. It is person-dependent. And lastly, the content of knowledge is *Brahman/Ātman* which is immutable (*kūṭastha*) and 'not what is to be accomplished through action (*asādhya*). The domain of ignorance is the unreal while the domain of knowledge is the real. They stand to one another as: the contradictor and the contradicted; the lion and the sheep; the sun and the night; the destroyer and the victim.

Now, mere action alone (*kevala karma*) cannot give liberation. This we have just determined. We shall proceed to show that even in combination, action cannot give liberation.[2] Action may be the means to knowledge (as an aid). But, so long as action is present, liberation has not been realized. When knowledge 'dawns', not only the means to it is no longer needed, but it cannot exist at all.

---

[2]Ibid., I.54.

III.ii. ACTION IS PRIMARY

Mīmāṃsā claims that action (*karma*) is primary and that knowledge (*jñāna*) is secondary. In their parlance, action is the *pradhāna* and knowledge is *guṇa*. However, Sureśvara objects to this position, and on three grounds. Firstly, according to Advaita, knowledge is the 'end' and action is the 'indirect means' thereto. This being the case, how can one claim that they exist together (in combination) at the same time? Their very relation is one of 'means and end' and, as such, this relation is not a combination at all. Secondly, if action is a means to knowledge and knowledge is a means to liberation, then it follows that together they cannot be the means to liberation. Finally, actions which are performed in a previous life can be the means to knowledge in a later life. If this is so, then the question of a combination cannot arise.

III.iii. ACTION AND KNOWLEDGE ARE EQUAL

As for the third option, i.e., the status of action and knowledge being equal in regards to liberation, this, too, cannot stand a close analysis. If action is what is sublated, and knowledge is the sublator, then where is the scope for a combination? Ignorance is opposed to knowledge. Further, ignorance is concerned with the unreal while knowledge is concerned with the real. Thus, even as light is opposed to darkness and can have no combination, so, too, knowledge is opposed to ignorance and can have no possible combination.

III.iv. A KNOWER'S RELATION TO ACTION

One who has secured the knowledge of *Brahman* is not subject to injunctions, either prescriptions or prohibitions. Why? "One who is free from the body (*videha*) is free from doubt (*vīta sandeha*) through the practice of 'not-this, not-this'."[3] Freedom from the body is freedom from both the gross and subtle bodies. Freedom from doubt is freedom from the causal body. When this occurs, one looks upon the psycho-physical organism as the non-self and pays no heed to their activity.

Sureśvara gives an analogy to exemplify this point:

> Just as a child imagines that his clay elephant is a real elephant and proceeds to play with it, so do the deluded people of the world super impose the body, etc. onto the Self and proceed to behave in various ways.[4]

Like in this example, conjunction between the imaginary and the real (or between action and knowledge) is admitted by the Advaitin in certain instances, i.e., in *mithyā-jñāna*. Another example is

---

[3]Ibid., I. 58.
[4]Ibid., I. 59.

given:

> When an individual takes the stump of a tree for a thief, he becomes frightened and runs away.[5]

Whenever knowledge functions as the prompter and action occurs for what is prompted, superimposition or false knowledge will occur.

However, right knowledge of *samyag-jñāna* does not lead to action. If an individual has right knowledge of the tree stump, flight will not be a logical consequence. Likewise, if an individual has right knowledge of the Self, such knowledge will never be a factor in an injunction to action. The Self neither acts nor is acted upon. To generalize this principle, since knowledge is opposed to action, knowledge cannot be found in conjunction with action. Those that are of a similar nature can co-exist, but not those which are of a different nature.

removed, not solely by knowledge, but through a long and continuous meditation upon the non-difference of the Self with *Brahman*. Thus, the central teaching of the *Upaniṣads* is not to be found in *mahāvākyas* like *tat tvam asi*, but in meditation upon the Self (*ātmetyevopāsīta*).[10] After one has studied the *mahāvākyas*, one must then meditate upon their purport. The upshot of the position is that a time interval elapses between the acquisition of liberating knowledge and the subsequent liberation.

The *sambandhokti* to verse 67 refers to two variations of the Mīmāṃsaka position. These two views have been identified by later commentators on the *Naiṣkarmyasiddhi* as belonging to Brahmadatta and Maṇḍana Miśra.[11] These views again surface in chapter III, verses 9-10, 89-93, and 119-126.

Brahmadatta says, in a nutshell, that even as there are injunctions in the *karma-kāṇḍa* of the *Vedas*, so too, injunctions appear in the *Upaniṣads*. Thus, the *Upaniṣads* enjoin meditation (*upāsana*) upon *Brahman/Ātman*. Assertive statements also exist, i.e., *satyam, jñānam, anantam*, but they are subsidiary to injunctive texts. What the Upaniṣadic texts convey (whether injunctive or assertive) is mediate knowledge (*parokṣa jñāna*). It is meditation upon these texts which will enable mediate knowledge to give rise to immediate knowledge. Direct knowledge (*sākṣātkāra*) removes ignorance. Thus, action (meditation) has to be performed in order to

---

[10] *Bṛhadāraṇyaka Upaniṣad* I.4.7.

[11] Jnanottama and Hiriyanna.

remove ignorance. It is action-cum-meditation, or, to state the entire position, *nitya-naimittika karmas* plus *upāsana* which yields liberation. Then, when the body falls off, the meditator will attain union with God.

It would appear that Brahmadatta's position implies that it is the practise of meditation plus action which removes ignorance. The text conveys indirect knowledge. With the aid of prescribed actions, along with meditation, this textual knowledge becomes immediate knowledge. But the question arises whether it is meditation (or, meditation cum action) which removes ignorance - or, is it the immediate apprehension (*sākṣātkāra*) which removes *avidyā*.

III.vii. MAṆḌANA

Maṇḍana's position is a slight variation of Brahmadatta's view. Both Maṇḍana and Brahmadatta are Vedāntins, but, according to Sureśvara, their tradition is not the true lineage (*satsampradāya*). Maṇḍana's view states that *Brahman* cannot be known directly through verbal knowledge (*mahā-vākya*) because words convey their meanings through complex sentences which involve multiplicity and internal differentiation. *Brahman* is non-dual and therefore cannot be known directly through the mere hearing of a Upaniṣadic text.

Maṇḍana's position may be conveniently summarized in a series of propositions:

1 - A sentence, by its very nature, can convey only relational knowledge (*saṁsṛṣṭa-viṣaya*).

2 - A sentence, by its very nature, can convey only mediate knowledge (*parokṣa-jñāna*).

3 - The *Upaniṣads* thus can convey only relational and mediate knowledge (*vākyārtha*).

4 - *Brahman* is non-relational and immediate and thus the *Upaniṣads* cannot directly convey *Brahman*.

5 - Knowledge from the *Upaniṣads* must be meditated upon in order to overcome this difficulty (*prasaṁkhyāna/ abhyāṣā/upāsana*).

6 - The results of meditation are immediate knowledge (*avākyārtha*).

7 - Immediate knowledge removes ignorance (*Bṛhadāraṇyaka Upaniṣad IV.iv.21* - *'vijñāya prajñām kurvīta'* - 'having known, one should attain that immediate knowledge').

8 - While practising mediation, one should also do *nitya* and *naimittika karmas* (they are not manditory, but they will help one for a quicker achievement). The analogy given is from the *Brahmasūtra* - one may take a horse or one may walk. Śaṅkara interprets the horse against *karma*/ for ploughing, while Maṇḍana interprets it for *karma*).

Sureśvara also refutes this position. The crux of the issue is not over the utility of mediation (which Sureśvara acknowledges as useful), but about the stage when meditation is needed. In other words, is meditation needed before or after the origination of *Brahman*-knowledge?

Sureśvara accepts the utility of meditation before the arisal of *Brahman*-knowledge. Mediation helps to remove the distractions in the form of doubt and/or erroneous cognition. Such distractions must be removed and meditation is an acceptable means of doing so. However, once the mind has become concentrated through meditation and *Brahman*-knowledge arises, mediation no longer is necessary. *Brahman*-knowledge, produced by the *śruti* text destroys ignorance and thus meditation, too, no longer has any scope for action.

III.viii ROLE OF SĀDHANA

In regards to spiritual practices (*sādhana*), Sureśvara acknowledges both external remote aids (*bahiraṅga-sādhana*) like *nitya-naimittika karmas* which will help purify the mind and external proximate aids (*antarāṅga-sādhana*) like the four-fold pre-requisites (*sādhana catuṣṭaya*). One cannot obtain *Brahman*-knowledge from these because, strictly speaking, one needs a valid means of knowledge (*pramāṇa*). These aids are only conducive to the origination thereof.

Thus, Sureśvara also knowledges the principal proximate aids (*mukya-antaraṅga-sādhana*) or *śravaṇa, manana,* and *nididhyāsana*. First, one should hear the text of which it has two parts: *avāntara vākyas* or subsidiary texts which do not give the liberating knowledge, and *mahāvākyas* or principal texts which give the liberating knowledge.

Śravaṇa or hearing the Upaniṣadic text removes any doubts that an aspirant may have in regards to the correct source of knowledge (*pramāṇa*). *Manana* or reflection removes any doubts one may have in regards to the correct object of one's knowledge (*prameya*). 'O.k., there is *Brahman* but what is this *Brahman* like, i.e., *saguṇa* or *nirguṇa*?' Finally, nididhyāsana or contemplation is for removing any errors or the 'opposite stream of thought' (*viparitabhāvanā*). It is for making the mind firm in its one-pointed fixity upon *Brahman*.

The *Upaniṣads* do not only teach the knowledge of *Brahman*. They also teach the oneness of the individual with that *Brahman* (*jīva-brahma-aikya*). Not only do they teach that *Brahman* is 'x', but also elevate the individual by teaching that when one knows 'x' correctly, one is 'x'.

While to maintain that meditation is necessary after the *mahāvākya* is heard is to question the very *pramāṇa* itself. One is questioning the source which is patently ridiculous. Before one hears, one can question and even meditate. But after the knowledge that the *mahāvākya* conveys arises, there is no longer any need to meditate.

CHAPTER FOUR

IV. NATURE OF THE SELF

IV.i. INTRODUCTION

Vedānta in general and Advaita in particular has often been designated or defined as the science of the Self (*Ātman-vidyā*). In the second chapter of his *Naiṣkarmyasiddhi,* Sureśvara makes a distinction between the Self and the non-self - both from the grounds of reason as well as from those of Scripture. He states some thirty-eight arguments to show how and why the Self is not the non-self.

IV.ii. SCRIPTURE

IV.ii.1. SCRIPTURE ONLY MEANS TO CONVEY KNOWLEDGE OF SELF

The knowledge conveyed by the six traditionally accepted means of valid knowledge (*pramāṇa*) falls into two categories: That which relates to the empirical world and that which relates to the trans-empirical reality.[1] All the six sources of knowledge, excepting 'words as knowledge' (*śabda*), relate solely to the empirical world. And of *śabda,* it consists of

---

[1] *Vedāntaparibhāṣā* VII, p. 150.

both that which is personal and conveys knowledge of the sensible and that which is impersonal and conveys knowledge of the supra-sensible.[2]

Perception is limited to the physical world. All the objects in the phenomenal world possess certain fixed characteristics such as grossness, fineness, name and form. But the Self is trans-empirical, trans-physical, trans-sensual and free from all distinctions. Thus perception can never reveal it. Inference, presupposes, and is dependent upon, perception. Comparison functions through a knowledge of similarity which presupposes difference and then relates the two or more relata. Postulation, too, presupposes difference. And non-apprehension, by its very definition, cannot give knowledge of the existent. Since the Self is ever-existent, trans-sensual, non-different, distinctionless, one and non-dual - it follows that these *pramāṇas* cannot reveal the ever-existent Self. Material senses can never reveal a non-material Reality. It should be obvious, therefore, that the senses are limited to the material sphere and that the Self can be known solely through the great statements of the *Veda*. "*Brahman* is known only through the Scripture" - "*sāstra yonitvat*".[3]

---

[2]Ibid., IV, p. 116.
[3]*Brahmasūtrabhāṣya* I.1.3.

IV.ii.2. OBJECTION - HEARD TEXT YET NOT UNDERSTOOD - 1

An individual has heard the great saying "that thou art" and yet that individual still doesn't understand or know the Self. How to explain this in light of what was just propounded?

IV.ii.3. REPLY - I

The answer to this objection occupies a major part of the second chapter of the *Naiṣkarmyasiddhi*. Basically, if an individual who has heard one of the *mahāvākyas* still does not understand the Self, it is because that individual does not understand the meaning of 'thou' or the 'Self'.[4] Is the Self: the physical body? the cognitive and conative organs? the mind? cognition? the void? the agent of actions and the enjoyer of fruits? a mere witness? or? We will explicate the nature of the Self, but first there are a number of minor objections which Sureśvara first introduces.

IV.ii.4. OBJECTION - HEARD TEXT YET NOT UNDERSTOOD - II

The next objection is perhaps the most obvious and common one made. Not everyone who reads the text and hears the *mahāvākya* obtains knowl-

---

[4]*Naiṣkaramyasiddhi* II.1.

edge of the Self. If it is merely, and exclusively, hearing one of the Great Sayings which produces enlightenment, then how is it that most individuals who the Great Sayings are not enlightened?

IV.ii.5. REPLY - NECESSARY PREREQUISITES - II

Like in every other religious system, Advaita Vedānta has certain conditions which must be fulfilled before understanding dawns. These are:

1 - Dispassion for the world (*vairāgya*)
2 - Longing for liberation (*mumukṣutva*)
3 - Approach a qualified teacher (*guru*)
4 - Association with a teacher leads to hearing a holy text
5 - Hearing a holy text leads to the *mahāvākya*
6 - Proper enquiry according to the method of agreement and difference (*anvaya/vyatireka*)
7 - Comprehension of the text
8 - Destruction of ignorance (*avidyā-nāsa*)
9 - Attain final goal of life (*puruṣārtha*)[5]

---

[5]Ibid. II.6-10.

IV.ii.6. OBJECTION - ŚRUTI NOT NECESSARY

Besides Scriptural statements, the objector states that there are a number of ways through which an individual may come to understand the 'Self'. The *pūrva pakṣin* claims that knowledge of the Self can be obtained without the aid of the *mahāvākyas* in the *Upaniṣads*. For instance:

1 - Virāj gained knowledge of the Self through mere reasoning;[6]
2 - Bhṛgu gained knowledge of the Self by remembering and reflecting upon its definition given by his father;[7]
3 - Śvetaketu gained knowledge of the Self by being told by his father;[8]
4 - The goblin (*pisācaka*) gained knowledge of the Self by accidentally hearing of it.[9]

These four examples are listed to demonstrate that historically there have been various ways in which individuals have come to understand the Self. They range all the way from a 'natural occurance' to a 'one-time accidental hearing' through a 'continuous pondering'. Thus, the

---

[6]*Bṛhadāraṇyaka Upaniṣad* I.4.2.
[7]*TaittirīyaUpaniṣad* III.1.
[8]*Chāndogya Upaniṣad* Chapter 6.
[9]*Sāṅkhyasūtrapravacanabhāṣya* of Vijñāna Bhikṣu IV.2.

question arises, 'aren't there ways in which an individual may become enlightened other than through the destruction of ignorance upon hearing and understanding the Vedic texts'?

IV.ii.7. REPLY

Sureśvara maintains that it is the text itself, and only the text, which produces knowledge of the Self. Any activity of an individual, either natural, accidental, or deliberate, is only an accidental aid thereto. *Mokṣa* does not come through action. Even if enlightenment appears to have arisen through some action, it is only the unseen and apparently hidden functioning of Scripture (which has been heard on some previous occasion) which must be responsible.[10]

In modern times, the same type of question was put to Ramana Maharshi.[11] 'How is it that you gained enlightenment without performing any spiritual practices?' The Maharshi answered, 'Obviously I must have performed many spiritual practices in a previous life.'

IV.iii PRAMĀṆA

The opponent then asks, 'how is it possible to ascertain the meaning of the *mahāvākyas* since the

---

[10]*Naiṣkarmyasiddhi* II.4.

[11]*See Collected Works of Ramana Maharshi.*

Self does not fall within the scope of any of the *pramāṇas*'? The 'I' is knowable as the mind-body complex by perception, etc. Thus, to declare that the 'I' is known as the Self by 'words as knowledge' and as the psycho-physical organism by the other valid means of knowledge is to set up a conflict between what the various *pramāṇas* reveal. And, if the Self is attributeless, it is unknowable by any *pramāṇa*. As well, you, yourself (the Advaitin) claim that 'it is purportful scripture that is authoritative, and not scripture as such'. If scripture were to proclaim something absurd or non-sensical, one should immediately reject such. "Even a hundred scriptural texts declaring fire to be cold or non-luminous will not attain authoritativeness."[12] Thus, you must reconcile this statement (the *mahāvākya* means that the Self is attributeless) with the obvious perception of the sense-organs which perceive the 'I' as a psycho-physical organism.

IV.iii.1. OBJECTION - SELF NOT WITHIN SCOPE OF PRAMĀṆA

The opponent then asks, 'how is it possible to assertain the meaning of the *mahāvākyas* since the Self does not fall within the scope of any of the *pramāṇas*'? The 'I' is knowable as the mind-body complex by perception, etc. Thus, to declare that the 'I' is known as the Self by verbal testimony and as the psycho-physical organism by the other valid

---

12 Śaṅkara's *Commentary* on the *Bhagavadgītā*, XVII.66.

means of knowledge is to set up a conflict between what the various *pramāṇas* reveal. And, if the Self is attributeless, it is unknowable by any *pramāṇa*. As well, you, yourself (the Advaitin) claim that 'it is purportful scripture that is authoritative, and not scripture as such'. If scripture were to proclaim something absurd or non-sensical, one should immediately reject such. "Even a hundred scriptural texts declaring fire to be cold or non-luminous will not attain authoritativeness."[13] Thus, you must reconcile this statement (the *mahā-vākya* means that the Self is attributeless) with the obvious perception of the sense organs which perceive the 'I' as a psycho-physical organism.

IV.iii.2. REPLY

The Scripture is distinctive in that what is known through it cannot be known through any other means. As well, there is no conflict between 'words of knowledge' and the other valid means of knowledge. Each is valid in its own sphere. Sureśvara says,

> Each of the valid means of knowledge has the inherent capacity to convey knowledge. Their intrinsic validity cannot be maintained in case one is regarded as complementary to another.[14]

---

13 Śaṅkara's *Commentary* on the *Bhagavadgītā* XVII.66.

14 *Naiṣkarmyasiddhi* III.86.

Sense perception is limited to the world of phenomena. As regards transcendental truths, Scripture is the sole valid source of knowledge.

> Only the empirical validity of perception and other allied means of knowledge is a proven fact; this is not controverted by the scriptures. What is controverted is its ultimateness, which is by no means a proven fact. Therefore there is no conflict between perception and the scriptures.[15]

As well, 'words as knowledge'. . .

> are true, not because it is a reliable person's statement (as the Naiyāyikas have it), but because the knowledge that it gives is uncontradicted. "The capacity of words to indicate a thing is intrinsically inherent in the words themselves and thus the truth of a statement is not dependent upon its maker. Thus, while a statement may be made based upon an individual's knowledge, its validity is its own and is not dependent upon the individual. In fact, Advaita maintains that all cognitions are intrinsically valid (*svataḥ-siddha*) and self-luminous (*svataḥ-prakāsā*).[16]

---

[15] *Advaitasiddhi,* Ch. 1, section 18 Bombay, Nirnaya-sagar Press, 1937, pp. 373-374.

[16] Grimes, *An Advaita Vedānta Perspective on Language,* p. Also see, *Vedāntaparibhāṣā* IV, p. 116.

IV.iv. DISTINCTION BETWEEN THE SELF AND NOT SELF - INFERENCE

IV.iv.1 BODY IS THE NOT-SELF - PRODUCT OF FOOD

Sureśvara begins a series of five inferences to demonstrate that the Self is not the physical body. His first argument deduces that the body is the not-self because it is a product of food (*annakāryatvāt*).[17] Whatever is produced must also decay, and thus the body cannot be the Self.

Thesis:	The body is the not-self
Reason:	It is a product (of food)
Example:	What is a product is the not-self, i.e., excreta
Application:	The body is a product (of food) which is invariably concomitant with the not-self
Conclusion:	Therefore, the body is the not-self

IV.iv.2 BODY IS THE NOT-SELF - NATURE OF FOOD

Again, the body is the not-self because it is of the nature of food (*āgantugatvāt*).[18] Before food is eaten

---

[17]*Naiṣkarmyasiddhi* II.11.
[18]Ibid., II.12.

and after it is rejected by the body, food is known to be other than the self. Thus, even in its in-between state, food should be recognised as being other than the self. Even as a garland or sandal paste is something which is different from oneself, so too is the body other than the Self.

Thesis:	The body is the not-self
Reason:	It is of the nature of food
Example:	What is of the nature of food is the not-self, i.e., a garland or sandal paste
Application:	The body is of the nature of food which is invariably concomitant with the not-self
Conclusion:	Therefore, the body is the not-self

IV.iv.3. BODY IS THE NOT-SELF - IT CEASES TO BE

Again, the body is the not-self because upon death it ceases to be (*apāyitvāt*).[19] So long as one dwells in one's body, one feels that one is the body. But once your body becomes a corpse and the dogs begin to fight over its remains, the body becomes an object of contempt. That which eventually dies,

---

[19]Ibid., II.13.

ceases to be, has an end. Thus, the body must be other than the Self.

Thesis:	The body is the not-self
Reason:	It is seen
Example:	What is seen is the not-self, i.e., like a jar
Application:	The body which is seen is invariably concomitant with the not-self
Conclusion:	Therefore, the body is the not-self

IV.iv.4 BODY IS THE NOT-SELF - IT IS SEEN

Again, the body is the not-self because it is seen (*dṛsyatvāt*).[20] Like a jar, the body is an object of perception. What is seen is different from the seer who sees it. Therefore, the body must be other than the Self.

Thesis:	The body is the not-self
Reason:	It is seen.
Example:	What is seen is the not-self, i.e., like a jar.
Application:	The body which is seen is invariably concomitant with the not-self.
Conclusion:	Therefore, the body is the not-self.

---

[20]Ibid., II.19.

IV.iv.5. BODY IS THE NOT-SELF - IT DOES NOT PERSIST

Again, the body is the not-self because it does not persist (*anavayāt*).[21] This is a variation of the third inference (IV.v.3.) except that Sureśvara gives another example. The body is perceived as an external object, like a pot, and its perceived continuity is broken (like dream-bodies which come and go).

Thesis:	The body is the not-self
Reason:	It does not persist
Example:	What does not persist is the not-self, i.e., like dream bodies which come and go
Application:	The body which comes and goes is invariably concomitant with the not-self
Conclusion:	Therefore, the body is the not-self

IV.v DISTINCTION BETWEEN THE SELF AND NOT-SELF - SCRIPTURE

IV.v.1. BODY IS THE NOT-SELF - CHĀNDOGYA UPANIṢAD

In support of Sureśvara's contention that the body is made of food and hence is not the Self, he

[21] Ibid.

refers to the *Chāndogya Upaniṣad* wherein it says, "Food becomes transformed into three parts as mind, muscle, and faeces".[22] Sureśvara draws an analogy between how one seed becomes threefold into chaff, grain, and straw and how eaten food becomes threefold as flesh, intellect, and excreta.[23]

IV.vi. DISCRIMINATE SELF FROM NOT-SELF

IV.vi.1. DESIRE AND AVERSION

To prove his point, Sureśvara gives an example to show that once an individual has correctly discriminated between the Self and not-self, desire and aversion no longer affect such an individual. "If an individual has voided excrement, and now considers such as impure, what will they care if others point out its impurity?"[24]

In a similar manner, once an individual has understood that the physical body is the not-self, what will such an individual care if others praise or criticize it? Once an individual has known that they are the immutable Self, what does it matter whether others praise or criticize? When this is accomplished, the bondage which derives from 'I' and 'mine' is cut.

---

22 *Chāndogya Upaniṣad* VI.5.1.
23 *Naiṣkarmyasiddhi*.II.15.
24 Ibid., II.16-17.

The Self must be discriminated from the not-self because:

1 - So long as body identification lasts, one can neither know the import of the *mahāvākyas* nor realize such.

2 - False knowledge (*mithyā jñāna*) differs from right knowledge (*viveka jñāna*). Even as a living individual thinks that the physical body the four pall-bearers know the heavy weight of the corpse. Thus, discriminatory knowledge knows the real weight of the body versus a false identification of the body which considers it light.

3 - The physical body no more belongs to the Self than does blueness belong to the sky.

4 - The notions of 'I' and 'mine' are no more properties of the Self than leanness or clothes are. They are objective and subject to cessation. (See *Bṛhadāraṇyaka Upaniṣad* I.5.1-3 *'annam brahma'*).

5 - Even as fire does not burn up in its own heat since heat is of its own nature, so too, if the not-self were the Self it could not be known as an object (since the two would not be distinct). However, the Self knows the not-self as an object and thus the two must be distinct.

IV.vi.2. OBJECTION - SELF IS BOTH SUBJECT AND OBJECT - I

The Bhāṭṭa Mīmāṃsakas raise an objection. They claim that the Self is an object of the ego-notion. They posit that the Self is both the knower and the known. On the basis of each individual's personal experience, they claim as proof the cognition 'I know myself'.

IV.vi.3 REPLY - I

Sureśvara replies that "that which is functioning as the object of a knowing subject cannot have that knower as its own object".[25] An object, *viz.*, a pot, cannot simultaneously be an object of knowledge and the knowing subject. Any entity which is an object of knowledge cannot be the knowing subject at the same time. Thus, he concludes that the ego-cognition cannot be both subject and the object.

To demonstrate why the 'I' is like a jar, Advaitin's use an enquiry into the three states of consciousness (*avasthā traya vicāra*). The Self or consciousness is present at all three levels or waking, dreaming, and deep sleep. However, the 'I' or ego-notion is present only at the first two levels. It is not present in the deep-sleep state. This proves that the 'I' is not the Self. When the mind is present, then the 'I' is present. When the mind is

---

[25] Ibid., II.24.

absent, the 'I' is absent. However, the Self is, by definition, omnipresent.

IV.vi.4. OBJECTION - SELF IS BOTH SUBJECT AND OBJECT - II

The Mīmāṃsakas continue their objection by stating that the Advaitin's reasoning process is incorrect. The Self is known as both the knower and the known through perception. It will not do for the Advaitin to raise an inferential reasoning process to refute perception since inference itself rests upon perception.[26]

IV.vi.5. REPLY - II

Sureśvara says that 'what is seen in a locus by a seer, is a quality that belongs to the locus'. For instance, in a red rose, the redness is seen in the rose (locus) and belongs to the rose (locus). Thus, the seer cannot be the seen; the knower is not the known.

This is a slight variation from Sureśvara's earlier replies. He has been demonstrating that the not-self is not of the nature of the Self; is not identical with the Self; is other than the Self; cannot know the

---

[26]All the Indian schools hold that inference is inferior to perception since inferences depends upon perception and cannot proceed without it.

Self. Now, he shows that the not-self does not belong to the Self; is not a quality of the Self.[27]

Jñānottama states that Consciousness or the knower or perceiver of the not-self (ego) is the witness-Self (*sākṣin*). The *sākṣin* is consciousness marked by the internal organ (*antaḥkaraṇa-upahita-caitanya*). It is always in relation to consciousness and the witness thereof. Even Sureśvara admits that the ego is given as an objective perception. What he denies is that the ego or not-self is the Self. Unlike the Mīmāṃsakas who believe that the Self can be given as an object of knowledge, according to Sureśvara the Self is knowledge itself and not an object thereof.

IV.vi.6. REPLY - III

Even if the not-self or ego were a quality of the Self, it would still be unknowable unless the Self could know itself as an object (which is impossible).[28] Furthermore, Sureśvara adds a further reply as to why the Self cannot know itself (or any quality therein if - such exists) as an object, *viz.*, the Self is partless, undifferentiated, and homogeneous.[29]

---

[27]*Naiṣkarmyasiddhi* II.25.

[28]Ibid., IV.vii.3 + 5.

[29]Ibid., II.26.

Sureśvara analyses the statement, 'I know myself', in three stages:

> 1 - At stage one, the Self is spoken of as a 'knower' (*jñāta*) to show a contrast between the Self and the not-Self.
>
> 2 - At stage two, the Self is not a 'knower' but know-ledge itself (*jñāna*).
>
> 3 - At stage three, the Self is said to be 'not-this, not this' (*neti neti*). In actuality, the Self cannot be described in words at all. "Words, along with the mind, return without reaching it."[30]

If the Self is said to know itself, there are two alternatives possible. Either: 1) The whole Self knows a part of itself, or 2) A part of the Self knows another part of the Self. But, neither of these cases present a viable solution because:

> i) If a quality inheres in a substance, it is not different from what it inheres in. Thus, it would not be possible for the Self to know itself since there would be no knower different from the known.
>
> ii) By definition, the Self is one and non-dual. Thus, there cannot be made a distinction between a substance and its qualities.
>
> iii) The Self is not made of parts.

---

[30]*Taittirīya Upaniṣad* II.iv.1.

iv) The Self is not an object of knowledge at all. According to Advaita, in order to be an object of knowledge there are two conditions which necessarily must be fulfilled. There must be a pervasion by a mental modification (*vṛtti vyāpyatva*) and there must be a pervasion by objectified knowledge (*phala vyāpyatva*). Yet, in regards to the Self, there is no objectified knowledge (*phala vyāpyatva*). Yet, in regards to the Self, there is no objectified knowledge since the Self is not subject to objectification.

v) Suppose one assumes for the sake of argument that the Self is something known - the question arises, 'who or what knows the Self?'. It would either have to be i) another Self or ii) the not-self.

But if a second Self knows the first Self, how is this 'second Self' known? One will land in an infinite regress with each prior Self having to be known by a subsequent Self. Or, if one says that the Self is known by the not-self, that plainly absurd, for, the not-self is by definition material and insentient and therefore can know nothing.

Thus, the Self is never an object of knowledge. The Self is the revealer of other things, of everything else, but it, itself, is never known by anything else. Nor can the Self be logically known in time (or at a later time). At one and the same moment, the Self cannot be both the seer and the seen, the knower and the known. And to posit an interval of time so that the Self can 'become' the known, the question again arises, who is the knower of this 'later' Self? Either *infinite regress* occurs or one must posit a not-self - of which both possibilities are absurd as we have just seen.

IV.vi.7. REPLY - IV

If the not-self or ego were really a part or property of the Self, then it would continue in deep sleep as well as after liberation. Yet, the 'I' is absent in deep sleep (as we observed earlier) and in liberation. If the 'I' were a quality of the Self, it would be present wherever the Self is. In reality, the 'I'-notion belongs to the inner organ (*antaḥkaraṇa*) and not to the Self.[31]

IV.vi.8. REPLY - V

As well, the Self is eternal. If the 'I' belonged to the Self, then the 'I' would also be eternal. This would render the Scripture futile. Not only would the Scripture's description of liberation be rendered void, but it would make its statements ridiculous concerning its exhortations to seek liberation.[32]

---

[31] *Naiṣkarmyasiddhi* II.32.
[32] Ibid., II.33.

IV.vi.9. REPLY - VI

The Self is immutable (*kūṭastha*); not subject to change (*avikari*). Thus, it is not a composite entity. The not-self is not a quality of it - even a changing quality. The colors of a mango change successively from seed to maturity, all the while fleetingly maintaining a reality as real as the mango itself. But the Self is not like a mango.[33] Sureśvara quotes, "There is no break in the sight of the Seer."[34]

When there is a change in a substance's attribute, it affects the character of the substance. A green mango is different from a ripe, red mango. Thus, the not-self cannot be a part of the Self. Since the not-self undergoes change, while the Self does not, the two cannot be related as substance and attribute.

IV.vi.10 OBJECTION - SELF IS BOTH SUBJECT AND OBJECT - III

The third objection raised regarding the status of the Self and the not-self posits that the Self need not be viewed as being eternal, permanent, unchanging, self-evident. Why not view the Self as the Buddhists do - as something ever-changing, in constant flux.

---

[33]Ibid., II.34.

[34]*Bṛhadāraṇyaka Upaniṣad* IV.iii.23.

IV.vi.11. REPLY - VII

Recognition and memory prove the fact that the Self is not the not-self. In order to know and recognize a series, the knower of the series must be outside of it. Memory presupposes the identity and persistence of the individual. It is one and the same individual who experiences objects and events and remembers them later on as having occurred to that individual. It is not as if one individual remembers another individual's experiences.

As well, there is the element of recognition. When an individual remembers an object, they recognize that they are remembering what they have previously seen. Hence, it is evident that the individual is not in constant flux.

Thus, we can conclude that one thing cannot at the same time be both seer and seen, Self and not-self. The seer cannot be seen by the object that is itself the seen. Nor can sight see the seer.

The not-self cannot belong to the Self even as heat and cold or light and darkness are mutually opposed to each other. The tip of the finger cannot touch itself nor can one climb onto one's own shoulders. If the seer is the seen, then the seer (Self) becomes an object of knowledge. And if everything is the seen, then who is the seer? The Self cannot be known by the not-self; nor can it be known by another Self; nor will it help to say that it doesn't know itself. Thus, we must conclude that the Self and the not-self are neither identical nor related in any way. Whether one invokes the *śruti,* i.e., *'Brahman* is *nirguṇa'*, or one invokes the *smṛti,* i.e.,

'The body is called the Field . . . wise people say that the Knower of the Field is one who watches what takes place within the body . . . know the Field is distinct from the Knower of the Field'[35], or one invokes reason, the not-self is different from the Self.

The world of the not-self has four qualities:

1 - falsity (*mithyā-siddha*)
2 - no definable essence (*anātmakam*)
3 - rooted in delusion (*moha-mūlam*)
4 - whose nature is inexplicable (*anirvacanīya*).[36]

If one asks how this not-self is shown to be false, Sureśvara answers that it is impossible to establish the existence of any real entity other than the Self. Therefore, the not-self is but a riddle, a sphinx which is impervious to all attempts to probe into its nature. "Wonder is its garment; inscrutable is its nature."[37] All enquiry into the not-self leads one into, and not out of, ignorance. It is on account of this puzzling nature that Advaitins call the not-self inexplicable.

---

[35]See *Bṛhadāraṇyaka Upaniṣad* III.viii.8; IV.ii.4 and *Bhagavadgītā* chapter XIII.
[36]*Naiṣkarmyasiddhi* II.44.
[37]*Pañcadaśī* VI.139.

IV.vi.12 THE ONE AND THE MANY

The Advaitin must explain how the One, non-dual Self appears as many. The Self is one. It is only through the multiplicity of objects that the one Reality appears to be many. Even as the one sun appears as many due to its reflection is various vessels of water, or, how one and the same individual is at the same time viewed as a friend, enemy, father, son, employee, etc. through the eyes of various individuals, so all distinctions in the one undifferentiated pure consciousness are due to its seeming associations with the physical world.

Sureśvara says, "Just as the sun is kidnapped by the waterpots and made to share their action, shape, and position, so is the Self appropriated by the multiple intellects of humanity".[38]

It is possible for a plurality of seemingly contradictory attributes to co-exist if they are not real. Thus a woman may invoke thoughts of beauty in the mind of a lustful man and thoughts of impurity in the mind of a monk and thoughts of tastiness in the mind of a dog - to use Sureśvara's example again.

The Self is 'One only, without a second'. No thought can be satisfied with less than the uncompromising primacy of the One as its ultimate truth. And only a non-dual One can be the unalterably fixed core underlying the universe of multiplicity. This is because the Self is consciousness. Consciousness can assume many forms without

---

[38]*Naiṣkarmyasiddhi* II.49.

endangering its non-duality. Even while being aware of the many, consciousness itself does not cease to be one. Everything is rooted in consciousness. And even after the myriad possible objects are elimanated, consciousness will still remain.

IV.vii. THE SELF

Verses 57 through 89 of chapter two of the *Naiṣkarmyasiddhi* can be taken as one unit as they are all devoted to delineating the nature of the Self. As Sureśvara says,

> The Infinite (*bhuman*), the partless, that which is actionless and not the factor of any action, the one that is beyond names and other categories - that self-revealed Self is the Self known by the Self-realized sages. That is the Self we teach.[39]

IV.vii.1. SELF AS SĀKṢIN

The first definition of the Self that Sureśvara gives is from an empirical point of view. If one presupposes that there are things-to-be-witnessed and duality is assumed then the Self is a witness (*sākṣin*). Note, however, that Sureśvara says, "as if through half-closed eyes."[40] This refers to the Self as That which witnesses the dance of every intellect

---

[39]Ibid., II.57.
[40]Ibid., II.58.

without the act of looking. The Self is not subject to change; it is only the mind which changes. Though the Self is said to be the witness, really it is not. Mental modifications come and go while the Self is permanent and unchanging. Their relationship is apparent and not real. To call the Self 'the witness' is but a contextual, a relative definition only.

IV.vii.2. OBJECTION - SELF IS NOT UNCHANGING

Quoting two Buddhist texts, an objection is raised that the Self is not unchanging.[41] The contention is that one is put between the horns of a dilemma regarding the question, 'Is the Self subject to change or not?' Common experience says that the Self changes, and, if this is the case, then the Self is, *ipso facto,* impermanent. On the other hand, if the Self is not subject to change, then this implies that the Self cannot be a knower.

A rather simple and almost purile example is given to show that the Self can neither be changing nor unchanging. If the Self is like the 'sky', then it cannot be a knower or experiencer (though it is unaffected by rain and sun). If the Self is like the 'skin', then it is mortal and impermanent (though rain and sun exert their influence upon it).

---

[41] Ibid., II.60-61.

IV.vii.3. REPLY - SKY AND SMOKE

Sureśvara responds to the opponent's objection with a counter-dilemma. He asks, 'when smoke rises into the sky, is the sky divided or not?'[42] The example seems to be both a subtle dig at the opponent's childish understanding and a reminder that subtle things like the sky and the Self are beyond the reach of action, change, and even differentiation.

> Therefore the ether can only be apprehended in itself as ether without reference to modifications and differentiations apparently introduced into it from without.[43]

For, if the sky is not divided (by the smoke), then the smoke cannot be rising. On the other hand, if the smoke is rising, the sky must be divided - but by what, for the smoke doesn't divide it. In a similar manner, when changes take place in the mind, the Self seems to be affected - but it is not (even as the sky is not affected by changes taking place within it).

IV.vii.4. REPLY - BOAT AND TREES

Even as it is erroneous to think that the Self changes when the world of multiplicity is superimposed upon it, so too, when a boat is

---

[42]Ibid., II.62.
[43]*Cāndrika*.

moving down a river, it is the boat that is moving and not the trees on the shore.[44]

IV.vii.5. REPLY - DIAMOND

Again, the Self is unchanged by changes which appears to happen within it, even as a diamond remains unchanged whether objects are reflected by its light or not. The radiant light of a jewel is said to illumine. But, the jewel is what it is, pure and brilliant, whether something is there to be illumined or not.

In a manner analogous to the jewel, the Self reveals every mind by its light (of consciousness). Whether there are objects there or not, the Self is what it is - ever-luminous and ever-present. If objects are nearby, they are revealed. If there are not objects, the Self remains what it always is.

Though, in actual fact the Self does not truly illumine. This is but a 'manner of speaking'. Figuratively speaking, from an empirical point of view, one says that illumination takes place due to the proximity of an object. But really speaking, it is but an 'appearance' for there is nothing truly real but the Self.

---

[44]*Naiṣkarmyasiddhi* II.63.

IV.vii.6. ADVAITA IS NOT SĀṄKHYA

It is the Sāṅkhya school which recognizes the Self as a witness (*sākṣin*).[45] There, both the Self (*puruṣa*) and what is witnessed/the not-self (*prakṛti*) are equally real. The changeless *puruṣa* witnesses the various changes which the *prakṛti* undergoes. But in Advaita, the Self alone is real and the not-self is unreal.

SĀṄKHYA	ADVAITA
- the world is due to *prakṛti*	- the world is due to *avidyā*
- the world is real	- the world is unreal (*mithyā*)
- the world in independent	- the world is dependent

Thus, unlike in Sāṅkhya, Advaita claims that the entire universe appears and disappears in the Self like clouds appearing and disappearing in the sky. The Self is not subject to change and any seeming duality does not touch the Self. It is the mind which seems to change and the Self remains untouched by it all.

---

[45] *Sāṅkhyakārikā*, verse XIX.

IV.vii.7. WHY THE MIND IS SUBJECT TO CHANGE

1 - The mind or the intellect (*buddhi*) is known to be subject to modification because it does not simultaneously know all things, past, present, and future. All empirical knowledge involves two factors: an unmoving reflection of intelligence (*cidābhāsa*) and a moving internal organ (*antaḥkaraṇa*). Since consciousness or the Self is known to be unmoving, it must be the intellect which is subject to change.

2 - The Self neither hears, sees, desires, feels pain, pleasure, hatred, anger, or any of the dualities. These are all properties of the mind. All of these changes come one after another (*krama dṛṣṭi*) and it is the mind which changes.

3 - The mind has a beginning and an end. Whatever possesses such attributes is subject to modifications.

4 - The Self is the witnesser of pain. Thus, pain must exist in the not-self, i.e., mind and body, because "a sufferer can never by the Witness, nor can the Witness be a sufferer."[46]

5 - There is an eternal stream of consciousness which flows regardless of the flux of pleasure and pain cognitions which come and go. it is the mind which has these partial cognitions (*katipaya dṛṣṭi*).

---

[46]*Naiṣkarmyasiddhi*, II.76.

And not only are these cognitions partial, but even at any given moment, one object is seen incompletely. Each mental cognition is different according to its object - but the light which illumines these various cognitions is the same.

6 - The Self is a witness to the presence and absence of all the fluctuations of the mind. Sometimes the mind functions and sometimes it does not. Sometimes one is awake, sometimes dreaming, and sometimes in deep sleep. The mind itself does not know, and cannot know that it functions thusly. Why? Because the mind cannot be both the knower and the known. As well, how can one have deep sleep if the mind can know itself? Deep sleep is defined as that condition wherein the mind does not function.

7 - The mind knows only that particular condition in which it happens to be in at any given moment. At that particular time it knows nothing else. This proves that it is subject to modifications. And if the mind is continually changing, it must be the Self that is the witness thereto. For, as we observed earlier, in order to cognize a series (of appearances and disappearances) there must be present a fixed immutable consciousness to witness such changes.

IV.vii.8. SELF IS ONE

> **The Self in the outcaste (*candala*) is one and the same as the Self in the Creator (*Brahma*). The one Light that exists in the two beings appears as many due to differentiations in the objects it illumines.[47]**

To say the the Self is here, in this place, and not there, in that place, is to miss it altogether. Neither the church nor the temple, the saloon nor the dance hall, the saint nor the sinner can exhaust it. No person, place, or thing has a monopoly on the Self.

An objection is raised at this point saying that, 'if the Self is one in all bodies, then an enlightened individual (*jīvanmukta*) must identify with the Self in all other bodies'. The consequences of this would mean that such an enlightened individual would be subject to every bound individual's sufferings.

Sureśvara remarks that such is not the case before enlightenment, so why should it follow afterwards. Before enlightenment occurs, one individual does not feel another's pain. Why should it be the case after *mukti*? The root cause of suffering is ignorance. When ignorance is destroyed, an individual is free from suffering. All along, the Self has never changed, much less suffered. In the case of a *mukta*, neither his body nor other's bodies are any longer considered real. Thus, a *mukta* is not subject to the sufferings of either his own body or

---

[47] Ibid., II.88.

the bodies of others. All pain is then known for the illusion it really is.

To support this conclusion, Sureśvara quotes the Vedic text: "Thou cannot see the Seer of seeing. With what, indeed, can one know the Knower of knowing?"[48] It is physical bodies which are subject to change and never the unchanging Self.

IV.vii.9. NATURE OF THE SELF

(1) The Self is: Free from all qualifications (*nirviśeṣana*). It is not a whole inclusive of parts.[49] There is nothing similar to it, nothing dissimilar to it, and it partakes of no internal variety.[50] It is different from the phenomenal, the spatial, the temporal, and the sensible.[51]

(2) The Self is: Not an object of knowledge (*aprameya*). The psycho-physical organism, as well as all physical objects, are known mediately. The mind is removed from the Self by one degree; the senses by two degrees; the body by three degrees; and the world by four degrees. But the Self is the Knower and not what is known. The existence of the mind, senses, body, world can be established only through empirical means of knowledge and proofs. Though the Self escapes objectification, it does not escape certainty. Nothing is more certain

---

[48] *Bṛhadāraṇyaka Upaniṣad* III.iv.2; II.iv.14.
[49] *Brahmasūtrabhāṣya* I.3.1.
[50] *Pañcadaśī* 2.20.
[51] *Brahmasūtrabhāṣya* IV.3.14.

than the fact of one's own existence. It is self-evident, direct, and immediate. No one is able to disbelieve in one's own existence. "A person may doubt of many things, of anything else; but one can never doubt one's own being."[52] This is because the very act of doubting would be but an affirmation of one's very existence. "It cannot be proved since it is the basis of all proof and is established prior to all proofs."[53]

What is mediate alone can be known through a *pramāṇa*. The Self is immediate. Therefore, the Self cannot be known through a *pramāṇa* and thus the Self is not an object of knowledge. The not-self needs to be established by another (consciousness plus an internal organ plus a valid means of knowledge) while the Self is self-established.

(3) The Self is: the basis of everything (*adhiṣṭāna*). The relation between the Self and the not-self is inexplicable (*anirvacanīya*). Traditionally there are three basic types of relationship:

1 - inseparable external relation (*samyoga*);
2 - inseparable internal relation (*samavaya*);
3 - identity (*tadatmya*).

However, the relationship between the Self and the not-self cannot be the first two types since these are possible only between two entities which are both real (the not-self is not real). And it cannot be the

---

[52]Ibid., II.3.7.
[53]Ibid.

third type for the Self and the not-self are not identical. Thus, though they are said to be related as the Revealer and the revealed, really speaking their relationship is inexplicable.

IV.vii.10 WHY NOT-SELF IS NOT REAL

The not-self is not real because:

1 - it cannot be established as real by itself (it is insentient);
2 - it cannot be established as real by the Self;
3 - it cannot be established as real by a combination of the Self and not-self since there can be no real relationship between them;

4 - it involves reciprocal dependency (*anyonyāśraya*). That is, difference or *bheda* can be acknowledged and accepted only if an individual already knows that there are two entities, 'a + b', and that 'a' differs from 'b' and vice-versa. However, to prove the reality of difference, one must prove that there are two entities and to prove that there are two entities, one must presuppose difference.

5 - it cannot exist separate from the Self.

IV.viii. SUMMARY - SELF AND NOT-SELF

The Self can be known by three criteria: self-established; attributeless; immutable.

1 - The Self, being of the nature of consciousness, is self-established. It is only by and through consciousness that anything is known. The internal organ, as well as the *pramāṇas* function only with the help of consciousness, though consciousness doesn't need the help of anything to be aware. In every act of knowing, consciousness must be presupposed. The not-self cannot know anything by itself because it is insentient. As well, mental modes are forever changing while consciousness is ever-present. A series can never be aware of itself as a series and needs a permanent witness outside of itself to know it.

2 - The Self is attributeless (*nirguṇa*). *Nirguṇa* means that the Self transcends the phenomenal realm. The Self is undefinable and, strictly speaking, unknowable - which means that it is too great for words to describe and the finite mind to fathom. All that can be known is the not-self - which is then superimposed upon the Self. It is only the seen or the known which can have attributes while the Self is beyond the relative concepts of unity or diversity.

3 - The Self is immutable (*kūṭastha*). It is that which presupposes phenomena. It is assumed as the foundation of all though it is not a substance in any sense of the word. Words denote things associ-

ated with either a certain genus, an act, a quality, or a mode of relation. But the Self does not belong to any genus. Its immutable and devoid of all attributes and relationships.

CHAPTER FIVE

V. INTERPRETATION OF MAHĀVĀKYA

V.i. INTRODUCTION

According to Sureśvara, the knowledge that one obtains from *śruti* texts like *tat tvam asi*[1] and *aham brahmāsmi*[2] is immediate and non-relational. Such texts signify the transcendental non-dual Reality. In another place I have maintained that within Advaita there is a tradition which claims that first-level expresions directly name the fact of the non-dual Absolute and second-level language symbolically, figuratively, and secondarily does so.[3] Here, our concern is with the ways in which Sureśvara interprets these texts.

Words convey their meaning through three kinds of signification, i.e., primary signification (*mukhya-vṛtti*), secondary signification (*lakṣaṇa vṛtti*), and signification based upon a knowledge of a similarity of qualities (*gauni-vṛtti*). As well, one must take into consideration the co-ordinate relation (*visesana-visesya-sambandha*) of the words in the text.[4] These are defined as follows:

---

[1]*Naiṣkarmyasiddhi* III.1-3; 5; 9-10; 22-29; 53; 75-80; 117-122.

[2]Ibid., II.28-29; II.54-56; III.39-40.

[3]See Grimes, *An Advaita Vedānta Perspective on Language.*

[4]See *Vedāntaparibhāṣā* IV. p. 93-102.

1 - PRIMARY SIGNIFICATION: A word used to convey a sense (through either a genus (*jati*), quality (*guna*), activity (*kriya*), or relation (*sambandha*) which exists in the sense that is conveyed.

2 - SECONDARY SIGNIFICATION: When the literal meaning of a text is unintelligible, then one or more of the words constituting it must convey some other meaning that is invariably connected with the primary meaning. There are three types:

> **1 - EXCLUSIVE:** *Jahallakṣaṇa* is when the implied meaning of a word of expression excludes the primary meaning. The implied meaning is other than, but nonetheless related to, the primary meaning which is comletely given up, i.e., in the sentence, 'the village on the river', the primary meaning of the word 'river' is completely given up and the bank or shore, which is related to the river, is implied.
>
> **2 - INCLUSIVE:** *Ajahallakṣaṇa* includes the primary meaning in the implied sense. Here, a meaning is implied which is other than the primary meaning of the word, yet which is related to it with the primary meaning not being given up, i.e., in the sentence, 'the school works today', the word 'school' indicates the members of the school. Thus, the primary meaning is maintained and included in the implied meaning.

3 - QUASI-INCLUSIVE: *Jahad-ajahal-lakṣaṇa* is when a part of the primary meaning of a word is given up and part of it is retained, i.e., in the sentence, 'this is that John', the meaning of the word 'this' refers to John as qualified by present time, place, etc., and the meaning of the word 'that' refers to the same John as qualified by past time, place, etc. The primary meanings of the two terms are incompatible. Thus, in quasi-inclusive implication, part, of the meaning of the words 'this' and 'that', *viz.*, the individual John, is accepted and another part of their meaning, *viz.*, 'as qualified by temporal and spatial aspects, etc.', is rejected.

3 - GAUṆĪ-VṚTTI: Signification based upon the knowledge of a similarity in qualities is when the literal sense of a sentence is unintelligible and one of the words in the sentence conveys some other meaning which has the same qualities that are present in its primary meaning. For instance, 'John is a lion' is unintelligible if it means that a man (John) is literally an animal (lion). But it makes sense to understand that John possesses the qualities of valour, cruelty, strength, etc. - the qualities which are present in the primary sense of the word 'lion'.[5]

---

[5]*Gauṇī-vṛtti* resembles *lakṣaṇā-vṛtti*. For their difference see Kumārila Bhaṭṭa's *Tantravārtika* or Sarvajñātman's *Saṁksepaśārīraka*.

4 - CO-ORDINATE RELATION: *Sāmānādhikaraṇya* is the grammatical principle which states that one entity may have two aspects, i.e., a 'blue lotus' has 'blueness' and 'lotusness'.

5 - SUBSTANTIVE-ATTRIBUTE RELATION: *Viśeṣaṇa-viśeṣya-sambandha* is the subject-predicate relation. The flower (lotus) is what is qualified by a color (blue).

This brings us to the heart of the matter. The Great Sayings appear to be unintelligible in their primary meanings. The word 'that' (*tat*) primarily refers to *Brahman* (which is omnipresent, omniscient, omnipotent, etc.) and the word 'thou' (*tvam*) primarily refers to the individual self (which is finite, limited, mortal, etc.). The same problem arises in regards to 'I' (*aham*) and *Brahman*. Thus, it is with the above stated interpretive tools that Sureśvara will attempt to overcome this dilemma and demonstrate that the Great Sayings do, in fact, coherently signify that *Ātman* is *Brahman*.

V.ii. AHAM BRAHMĀSMI

V.ii.1. AHAM BRAHMĀSMI - I

In the text, 'I am the Absolute' (*aham brahmāsmi*), the opponent claims that 'I' refers to one's ego-nature on the grounds of grammatical co-ordination (*samanadhikaranya*).[6] Just as their is grammatical co-ordination between the words 'I' and 'fair' in

---

[6]*Naiṣkarmyasiddhi* II.28.

the expression, 'I am fair', so too, there is grammatical co-ordination between 'I' and 'Absolute'.

Sureśvara replies that grammatical co-ordination need not imply identity. There are two types of grammatical co-ordination: co-ordination in the sense of sublation (*bādhāyām sāmānādhikaraṇya*) and co-ordination in the sense of oneness (*aikye sāmānādhikaraṇya*). One must employ this grammatical principle carefully. In the expression, 'I am fair', 'fairness' is a characteristic of the body, but, the body is not 'I'.

Sureśvara interprets this *mahāvākya* by means of the grammatical principle, co-ordination in the sens of sublation.[7] He gives the example of the judgement, 'this post is a man'.[8] In one's earlier judgement, one believes that an object (a man) is a post. But a subsequent judgement, upon closer scrutiny, reveals that it is post. Likewise, one's original judgement believes that the 'I' refers to one's ego-nature, while a subsequent judgement sublates this earlier view and reveals that 'I' is the Absolute. Upon realization, the ego-nature is sublated. The 'I' with adjuncts is not the Self; the 'I', in its essential nature, is the Self.

---

[7]Ibid., II.29.

[8]See *Pañcadaśī* VIII.42f. and *Siddhāntaleśasaṅgraha* I.34 where this verse is discussed.

V.ii.2. AHAM BRAHMĀSMI - II

Sureśvara demonstrates another way in which to interpret this *mahāvākya*.[9] In its primary (*mukhya* or *prasiddha vṛtti*) meaning, 'I' equals one's ego-nature. Because this primary meaning is unintelligible, one must resort to a secondary meaning (*lakṣaṇā vṛtti*). The type of secondary meaning that Sureśvara invokes here is exclusive or *jahallakṣaṇā*. The primary maning of 'I' (consciousness with attributes) is completely given up and a secondary meaning (consciousness without attributes), other than but nonetheless related to the primary meaning, is accepted.

V.ii.3. AHAM BRAHMĀSMI - III

Sureśvara demonstrates that there is still another way in which *aham brahmāsmi* can be interpreted.[10] There exists a similarity between the Self and the ego. Both have the common qualities of subtlty, inwardness, and behave as if they are the perceiving Self. On this account, one may nterpret the text by means of signification based upon the knowledge of similarity of qualities (*gauṇī vṛtti*). Thus, the Self is implied by a word ('I') which primarily refers to the ego - even though the ego is material and insentient and cannot be equated with *Brahman*.

---

[9]*Naiṣkarmyasiddhi* II.54.
[10]Ibid., II.55.

V.ii.4. AHAM BRAHMĀSMI - IV

Finally, Sureśvara interprets *aham brahmasmi* directly or in a primary sense to mean 'I' am the 'Absolute' on the strength of the knowledge that the ego-notion cannot exist without the Self.[11] All that is not the Self, is not Consciousness, is not-real and therefore cannot even appear to exist without the aid of the Self. Thus, in a peculiar and interesting twist, 'I' (or any word for that matter) must refer to the constitutive being of anything whatsoever and as such designates that which is self-evident, immediate, direct, and certain, i.e., the Self.[12]

Thus, the word 'I' may be applied to the Absolute by:

1) grammatical co-ordination in the sense of sublation (II.28);
2) indirect exclusive usage (II.54);
3) figurative usage (II.55);
4) primary meaning (ii.56).

Sureśvara shows considerable ingenuity by demonstrating that whatever sense one chooses to take the word 'I' to man, whether primary, secondary, or figurative, the text is in any case intelligible.

---

[11]Ibid., II.56.

[12]This is the central topic of An *Advaita Vedānta Perspective on Language*.

V.iii TAT TVAM ASI

V.iii.1 TAT TVAM ASI - I

According to Sureśvara, the knowledge which is derived from *tat tvam asi* is immediate and non-relational. Normally sentences are relational and yet we will observe that a relational sentence, *tat tvam asi,* will give a non-relational meaning. The relational, verbal sense (*vākyārtha*) of the text will give a non-verbal, unitary, impartite meaning (*avākyārtha*). Sureśvara is fond of emphasizing that non-relational *Brahman*-knowledge arises from a relational sentence.

There are three steps/considerations which must be taken into account in the understanding of a *mahāvākya:*

1 - **GRAMMATICAL CO-ORDINATION** (*sāmānādhikaraṇya-jñāna*): This is the grammatical co-ordination or relation which exists between two terms, i.e., 'blue lotus' or '*tat tvam asi*'.

2 - **SUBJECT-PREDIATE RELATION** (*viśeṣana-viśeṣyata-jñāna*): This is knowledge which has a subject-predicate relation.

3 - **INDIRECT IMPLICATION** (*lakṣya-lakṣaṅa-sambandha-jñāna*): This is implied meaning inherent in the terms of a statement.[13]

---

[13]*Naiṣkarmyasiddhi* III.3.

Now, a sentence sense (*vākyārtha*) can be of two kinds:

1 - **RELATION OF DUALITY** (*bheda-samsarga*):

In which the meaning of a sentence is conveyed through a relation obtained among the words conveying the difference, i.e., 'bring the cow with a stick' (wherein, from the usage of the various words, difference is known - stick/cow/bring/etc.

2 - **RELATION OF NON-DUALITY** (*abheda-saṁsarga*):

In which oneness is known through the relation of the words, i.e., 'blue-lotus' or '*tat tvam asi*'. This is of two kinds:

i - **RELATION WITH ONENESS** (*saṁsarga abheda*):

In which there is oneness with relation; the object is one though it has multiple meanings/attributes.

ii - **IDENTITY STATEMENT:** (*svarūpa abheda*):
In which a non-relational sentence in which two entities referred to are actually identical/one.

Before we actually observe how Sureśvara interprets the *mahāvākya 'tat tvam asi'*, it should be noted that an understanding of a *mahāvākya* involves a two-fold benefit. Even in an empirical statement which involves grammatical co-ordination, there is this two-fold benefit. For instance, in the statement, 'blue lotus', both the color 'blue' benefits as well as the flower 'lotus'. The idea of 'blueness' removes all other possible colors from the lotus and 'that' which is blue is precisely a 'lotus'. Thus, each is enriched and benefits from their association.

In a similar manner, *'tat'*, by its association with *'tvam'* removes the misconception that it is remote, unattainable, hidden, etc., and reveals itself as that which is ever-manifest, immediate, direct, and the inner-most Self. In a similar manner, *'tvam'*, in its association with *'tat'* removes the misconception that it is mortal, finite, bound, and imperfect and reveals itself as that which is self-existent, ever-pure, ever-free, and immortal. Thus, what was conceived of as the farthest of the far is revealed as nearer than the nearest; what appeared to be unattainable is already attained; what is ever hidden is really self-manifest.[14] Or, as Gauḍapāda said, "This view (that there is duality) is only for the sake of instruction. When the truth is known, all this duality is gone."[15]

Now, according to Sureśvara, there are three steps or considerations to take in interpreting the meaning of *'tat tvam asi'*:

1 - **SĀMĀNĀDHIKARAṆYA**: The connotations of the two terms 'That' and 'thou' are different. 'That' refers to *Brahman* which omnipotent, omnipresent, omniscient, etc., and 'thou' refers to the individual self which is finite, bound, limited, etc. When the meanings of two words are different, one usually thinks that their denotations are also different. However, where there is grammatical co-ordination in a sentence, the things referred to are not different. The words 'That' and 'thou' are in grammatical co-ordination and thus refer to the same object, even as 'blue' and 'lotus' refer to the same object.

2 - **VIŚEṢAṆA VIŚEṢYA SAMBANDHA**: In order to do justice to the different connotations of, and the co-ordinate relation between, these two terms, Sureśvara invokes the subject-predication relation. In the expression, 'the blue lotus', one object is denoted while, being a flower, also possesses a blue color. Thus, though the two terms have different connotations, they have the same denotation. This

---

[14] See *Muṇḍaka Upaniṣad* III.1.7-8.

[15] *Māṇḍūkyakārikā* III.18.

way of construing the meaning is known as 'identity which involves relation' (*abheda-saṁsarga*).

3 - **LAKṢYA LAKṢAṆA SAMBANDHA:** There is a difficulty involved in interpreting *'tat tvam asi'* by *abheda samsarga*. It works well with 'the blue lotus' because there is a 'subject-predicate relation'. But with the *mahāvākya*, there is an identity wherein 'Thou' cannot be an attribute of 'That'. Thus, one must apply the relation of non-duality (*svarūpa abheda*). It would be unintelligible to identity 'That' with 'thou' in view of the fact the determinants of the two terms are mutually incompatible. In other words, this statement cannot be treated as an attributive judgement. The import of the statement is identity - but not a relational identity. Thus, the non-relational meaning of the text can only be revealed by a re-course to its implied meaning. Thus, according to Sureśvara,

> On our view, the relations such as *sāmānādhikaraṇya* (which connect words and their meanings) directly bring out the non-verbal import of *'Tat tvam asi'* like the identity of ether through the cancellation of the different adjuncts.[16]

What he has emphasized is that, in employing the secondary meaning of the terms in the *mahāvākya*, he has removed the incompatible determinants of

---

[16]*Naiṣkarmyasiddhi* III.9. The sentence, 'the ether in the pot is the ether in the sky' is unintelligible without referring to the ether without any limiting adjuncts or qualifications.

each term. By removing omniscience, omnipotence, etc., from 'That' and by removing limitedness, boundness, fallibility, etc., from 'thou' - while retaining the common element between them, i.e., consciousness, he has demonstrated that *tat tvam asi* conveys a sense of non-relational identity.

Some implications from this interpretation include: What we usually associate with 'thou' (suffering, etc.) is cancelled by its association with 'That' and what we usually associate with 'That' (remoteness, etc.) is cancelled by its association with 'thou'.[17]

CHAPTER SIX

VI. SCRIPTURE

VI.i. INTRODUCTION

In the *Naiṣkarmyasiddhi,* Sureśvara analyses Scripture under various topics:

1 - Definition and Scope;
2 - Work;
3 - Relation (to other *pramāṇas);*
4 - Status.

VI.ii. DEFINITION AND SCOPE

Sureśvara states that no other valid means of knowledge, excepting the Scripture, can impart knowledge of supra-sensible facts:

> The knowledge of the inmost Self which removes all need for further investigation arises with certainty from the texts like 'That thou art'. It does not arise from any other means of knowledge.[1]

---

[1] *Naiṣkarmyasiddhi* III.67.

Perception is limited to the empirical world. All the things of the phenomenal world possess certain fixed characteristics such as grossness, fineness, etc. Name and form are their warp and woof. But the Self is trans-empirical, trans-sensual, and free from all distinctions.[2]

Inference presupposes, and is dependent upon, perception (according to Indian philosophy). For a valid inferential cognition there must exist the knowledge of an invariable relation between the middle and the major terms as well as the middle term must also be perceived as existing in the minor term. Thus, it is obvious that inference, though an independent source of knowledge, is dependent upon perception and therefore, like perception, restricted to the empirical world of sensible objects.[3]

Knowledge involves the triple factor (*tripuṭī*) of: cognizer, object cognized, and the means of cognition. But the Self does not fall within the scope of knowledge as an object of knowledge. Sureśvara said, "Because the entire mechanism of knowledge relates to the external world, as far as one can understand, the ordinary modes of knowledge are only for producing knowledge of external objects."[4]

Thus, Sureśvara puts forward various reasons why perception and the other valid means of

---

[2]See ibid., III.48.
[3]Ibid., III.51.
[4]Ibid., III.52.

knowledge cannot reveal the Self. He sums up his position by saying,

> As the Self is of the nature of eternal awareness, as it stands in need of no other proof, as it is without physical qualities, as it is that about whose existence doubts can never arise, as it is the inmost Self, as it is an end in itself, as it is not an object of knowledge, it is not cognized through the valid means of knowledge like perception, etc.[5]

Śruti is superior to the other *pramāṇas* with regards to super-sensuous facts. In matters that are sensuous, however, Scripture is not the primary means of knowledge. Even a thousand scriptural injunctions cannot convert a hat into a rabbit.

Why would anyone not accept the authority of the Scripture? Four reasons are advanced by Sureśvara in this regards.[6] These are:

1 - Restatement
2 - Contradiction
3 - Doubtful
4 - Uninformative

1 - The first objection against the *śruti* is that it is merely a restatement (*anuvāda*) of what is already known. However, this objection fails on two counts. First, by definition, as *pramāṇa śruti* conveys knowledge which is not otherwise known. Purport

---

[5]Ibid., III.47-48.
[6]Ibid., III.35-37.

(*tātparya*), which signifies not only the meanings of individual words, but also the relation among the meanings of the words syntactically conjoined, distinguishes Scripture as an independent means of valid knowledge. Secondly, while perceptions say that an individual is limited, bound, and finite, Scripture says that the individual is unlimited, ever-free, and bliss.

2 - The second objection against sruti is that its information is contradicted by other *pramāṇas*. However, this objection fails to take into consideration that two *pramāṇas* can contradict each other only in regards to the same subject matter. But *śruti* is a means of knowledge regarding super-sensuous matters and perception, etc. are means of knowledge regaarding sensuous matters. Thus, they have a different subject-matter (*bhinna viṣaya*).

3 - The third objection *śruti* is that its information is doubtful Is this doubt due to: i) a defect in the *pramāṇa* or ii) a defect in the object (*prameya*)? In order for a *pramāna* to b considered a *pramāṇa*, it cannot give doubtful information (*pramā karaṇam pramāṇam*). Thus, it must be the objects of the world which have room for doubt. But, the Self is immediate and in regards to it there is no room for doubt. It is immediate and certain.

4 - The fourth objection against *śruti* is that it conveys no information at all. Sureśvara agrees if only the individual involved is an idiot, a dull lump of clay. Otherwise, *śruti* conveys knowledge of

the Self to those individuals who are fit or eligible (*ādhikārin*).

VI.iii. WORK (How does *śruti* convey knowledge of *Brahman/Ātman?*)

How does *śruti* convey knowledge of *Brahman* or the Self? Sentences are said to give knowledge of their meaning through the knowledge of the meanings of the words which constitute them. Thus, if one knew the meaning of the words *'tat'* and *'tvam'*, one should know what *'tat tvam asi'* means.

Earlier (chapter five) we observed that words cannot signify the super-sensuous directly. A word is said to convey a primary signification when its meaning is conveyed through either a genus (*jāti*), quality (*guṇa*), activity (*kriyā*) or relation (*sambandha*). Since the Self/*Brahman* does not posses any of these media, it is usually said that words cannot signify the Self/*Brahman*.

Another reason for advancing that words do not convey knowledge of *Brahman/Ātman* is that there is no knowledge of the significative relation between the words and *Brahman/Ātman*. The significative sense of a word is known through perception, etc., by the mind. But in the case of *Brahman/Ātman*, there is no external object which the mind can know. Since *Brahman/Ātman* is not known by the mind, it also has no significative relation of words which pertains to it.

Thus, one generally resorts to a secondary meaning of words in order to explain what, at first glance, appears unintelligible. In all, there are six different methods which the Advaitin employes to convey Self-knowledge linguistically.[7] These are: the technique of prior superimposition and subsequent denial (*adhyāropa* and *apavāda*); *via negativa*; secondary implication (*lakṣaṇa*); direct hearing (*śravaṇa*); etymology; and silence. However, in the *Naiṣkarmyasiddhi*, Sureśvara mainly explores secondary implication with one reference to direct hearing.

It should be noted however, that even though words are generally said to 'return, along with the mind, without reaching it', the Self is known. Śaṅkara said, "*Brahman* is not a non-object in an absolute sense."[8] Why? It is the object of the notion of the ego and thus is immediately known by everyone. No one says that 'I' do not exist and to say such would be self-contradictory. Thus, the 'I'-notion proves that *Brahman/Ātman* is not unknown entirely.

The Scripture does not seek to establish the Self as an entity referable objectively by the word `this'. Its aim is to remove the ignorance which imagines and superimposes on the Self, differences. When knowlege of *Brahman/Ātman* occurs, not only is ignorance destroyed, but also the apprehending consciousness which is included, ontologically, in ignorance, and is a product of it. Thus, the Self may

---

[7] See my *An Advaita Vedānta Perspective on Language.*

[8] *Brahmasūtrabhāṣya* I.1.1 *'na tāvadayam ekāntenāviṣayaḥ'.*

be said to be known, and yet, there is no knower, no known, and no knowledge in such a situation. "Through what should one know that owing to which all this is known?"[9]

VI.iv. RELATION (to the other *pramāṇas*)

There is no conflict between the Scripture and the other means of valid knowledge. We have already touched upon this earlier. The most telling argument of Sureśvara is that their subject-matter differs.[10] All the means of knowledge besides Scripture have as their ground and result multiplicity/duality/difference. But the Scripture teaches non-duality as its purport.

If an objection is raised that Scriptural statements are existential and thus cannot convey anything without an injunction, the answer is that even a descriptive statement conveys knowledge and as knowledge, removes ignorance. Therefore, it is gratuitous to declare, like the Mīmāṃsakas do, that knowledge about an established fact is meaningless without the support of an injunction.[11]

---

[9] *Bṛhadāraṇyaka Upaniṣad* II.4.14.

[10] *Naiṣkarmyasiddhi* III.44-45.

[11] Ibid., *sambandha* to III.47. The example is given that existential statements have the same authority as a sentence used to awaken a sleeping individual. That is, the words with which one awakens a sleeping individual are not (for that individual) an authoritative means of knowledge for any object in the empirical world, however they are authoritative in waking him up to a new state of consciousness.

As we observed in the previous chapter, the Self doesn't fall within the scope of perception, etc. The reasons for this include:

1 - the Self is immutable consciousness;
2 - the Self does not need the help of perception, etc;
3 - the Self doesn't have physical qualities (*nirguṇa*);
4 - doubt is not possible in regards to the Self;
5 - the Self is an end in itself;
6 - the Self is not an object of knowledge.

Since the Self is not within the scope of perception, etc., it follows that it is knowable by means of *śruti* alone.

Scripture is the only valid means of knowledge which does not depend upon perception at some stage or other. All the other *pramāṇas* thus presume a relationship while the Self is relationless.

For the sake of argument, even if a conflict exists between the Scripture and the other valid means of knowledge, the Scripture is final. Why? Because the Scripture is authorless (*apauruṣeya*). Thus it is free from defects, either human or divine. All the other valid means of knowledge are conditioned by other factors like perception, etc. They have been known to mislead in the past, and are likely to do so in the future. For instance, perception has given contradictory knowledge. During the state of sleep, one thinks of oneself in bliss. Yet during one's waking state, perception shows the self to be bound, in pain, etc. If this is the case, then perception, etc. may mislead one in the future too.

The relation of Scripture to reason is one in which reason supports Scriptural statements. There are numerous examples, i.e., in the *Chāndogya Upaniṣad* wherein Indra and Virocana learn from Prajāpati through an enquiry into the three states of existence. Or, in the *Bṛhadāraṇyaka Upaniṣad* wherein Yājñavalkya tells Janaka to go deeper and deeper in his enquiry into 'what is the light?'.

VI.v. RELATION OF SCRIPTURE TO REASON

Sureśvara does not deny the relation which exists between *śruti* and reason. In a number of places he states that reasoning must be employed to aid in discriminating the Self from the not-self.[12] Though reason is ancillary to Scripture, it is important and must not be overlooked because it helps to both clarify the issues raised by Scripture and to assist in rendering the teachings of the Scripture intelligible. Without reasoning, the purport of the *mahāvākyas* will not arise - even though mere reasoning by itself will not be sufficient. Thus, reasoning may be said to be necesary, though not sufficient, in understanding Scripture.

Reason, however, has its limitations.

---

[12] *Naiṣkarmyasiddhi* III.33; 63; IV.15.

1 - It lacks certitude as it is only capable of giving mediate knowledge which must eventually be validated through some other knowledge.

2 - There is no finality in respect of its conclusion since what is reasonable from one point of view or perspective may be untenable from another.

3 - Reason gives only relational knowledge. All mental cognitions involve the duality of subject and object, substance and attribute, etc. But the Self is non-relational and thus cannot be known exclusively through reason.

4 - Reason can tell what the not-self is and even help discriminate the not-self from the Self, but it can never tell what the Self itself is.

5 - The Buddhists relied exclusively on reasoning and thus were led astray. Without the assistance and guidance of the *śruti,* there is a danger involved in reasoning in that reason can prove any-thing to be the case. Left to itself, reason can prove any number of inconceivable things.

6 - Another danger of reason is that an intelligent person can defeat someone less intelligent. A clever, quick intellect which has a defective understanding may still prove itself right in the face of someone with a slow, illogical mind whose under- standing is nevertheless correct.

7 - Finally, one cannot bring all of the logicians of the past, present, and future together in order to decide the entire ramifications, permutations, and combinations of logic. Thus, one will never know what the last word in logic is.

8 - In an inferential process, knowledge of the invariable relation between the middle and major terms (*vyāpti jñāna*) is necessary. In order to derive the *vyāpti jñāna*, the minor term (*pakṣa*) must be perceived. Then one needs to know the relation of the minor term to the middle and major terms. But how is one to get this relation when *Brahman/Ātman* is imperceptible and has no relationships whatsoever?

All this not withstanding, reason has a number of excellent qualities:

1 - It is needed even to criticize itself.
2 - It is needed to interpret the Scripture.
3 - Scripture itself accepts it.

VI.vi. STATUS

According to Advaita, *Brahman/Ātman* alone is real. The means to the knowledge of *Brahman/Ātman* is *śruti*. Thus the question arises, 'what is the ontological status of *śruti?*' If it is real, then the non-duality and central tenet of Advaita is destroyed. On the other hand, if it is unreal, then what is revealed by an unreal means of knowledge should also be unreal. The words of a liar do not lead to the truth.

Advaita accepts the ontological unreality of Scripture. However, it still maintains that Scripture, an unreal epistemological device, is the source and means for knowledge of the metaphysical Reality. To render this clearer it is necessary to distinguish between the ontological status of Scripture and its status as a valid means of knowledge. One aspect does not affect the other and the criteria of one is not the criteria of the other.

Knowledge is held to be valid if it is unsublatable. As *Brahman/Ātman* is eternal, immutable, and therefore unsublatable, knowledge of *Brahman/Ātman* as given by Scripture is valid. This means that it is not necessarily true that what is revealed by an unreal means of knowledge must also be unreal. In fact, numerous instances can be cited to demonstrate that a non-real entity can give rise to valid knowledge. For instance, a lion roaring in a dream is an illusory animal and yet, it enables the dreamer to awaken from the dream. Likewise, a snake drawn on a piece of paper is not a real snake and yet, from one's perception of this 'paper-snake', knowledge of a real snake may be conveyed. Or again, the cognition of a 'rope-snake', which is not-really a snake, can give rise to fear, perspiration, trembling, even death, which are real.

Thus, Sureśvara declares that when the final truth of non-duality is realized, Scripture also becomes non-existent (*yatra vedāḥ avedāḥ*). The Scripture is intended as a methodological device by means of which individuals who dwell in ignorance may dispell such. It is meaningful and useful only to unenlightened individuals and ceases to have value and use for one who has *Brahman*-knowledge.

CHAPTER SEVEN

VII. THE LOCUS OF AVIDYĀ

VII.i. INTRODUCTION

The question raised in the *sambandha* to the third chapter of the *Naiṣkarmyasiddhi* concerns the locus (*āśraya* and content *viṣaya*) of ignorance (*avidyā*). Śaṅkara did not raise this question polemically. The generally held idea is that Śaṅkara conceived of *Brahman/Ātman* as both the locus and content of *avidyā*. This idea stems from the fact that there are several places wherein he refused to answer the question, 'whose is *avidyā*?', on the basis that to do so would imply that *avidyā* was real.[1]

Sureśvara was the first Advaitin to raise this question. Although all Advaitins subscribe to the doctrine of non-duality, they differ in their mode of expounding such. After Śaṅkara, either by way of a sub-commentary (*vārttika*), or a gloss (*tika*) on Śaṅkara's *bhāṣyas*, there arose two distinct schools or traditions (*prasthāna*) of thought within the Advaita lineage: the Bhāmatī and the Vivaraṇa. The Bhāmatī *prasthāna* has its roots in Maṇḍana and flowered in Vācaspati's *Bhāmatī*. The

[1]See *Upadeśasahasrī* XVIII.44f. and *Bhagavadgītābhāṣya* XIII.2.

Vivaraṇa *prasthāna* has its roots in Sureśvara and flowered in Prakāśātman's *Pañcapadikavivaraṇa* and Vidyāraṇya's *Vivaraṇaprameyasangraha.*[2]

No doubt these two schools differ in their interpretation of certain aspects of Advaita doctrine. However, it can never be stressed enough, and it must always be remembered, that these differences are of an exegetical and not doctrinal nature. Both of these schools are based upon, and owe allegiance to, Śaṅkara. In their attempts to clarify, elucidate, and respond to contemporary objections to Advaita's philosophical position, these differences arose. And yet, in the view of Sureśvara, these relative perspectives are intended only to help us realize the inward Self.[3] This is their real significance.

Maṇḍana argued in favor of a view that the individual self (*jīva*) should be regarded as the locus (*āśraya*) of *avidyā*. Further, since this *avidyā* obscures the essential nature of *Brahman, avidyā* has *Brahman* as its object (*viṣaya*). Sureśvara vehemently opposed any degree of differentiation between the locus and content of *avidyā* and maintained that *Brahman* itself is both (the locus and content of *avidyā*).

---

[2] Amalananda's *Kalpataru* (a *Commentary* on the *Bhāmatī*) and Appayya Dīkṣita's *Commentary* on the *Kalpataru* are other works in the Bhāmatī tradition. Padmapāda's *Pañcapādikā* commences the Vivaraṇa line.

[3] *Bṛhadāraṇyaka-upaniṣad-bhāṣya-vārtikā,* I.iv.402. *yayā yayā bhavetpuṁsāṁ vyutpattiḥ pratyagātmani sā saiva prakriyeha syāt sādhvī sā cānavasthitā.*

This disagreement served as the basis for the later distinction which came to be known as the Bhāmatī-Vivaraṇa distinction. It grew when Vācaspati, in his commentary on Śaṅkara's *Brahmasūtrabhāṣya* (called the *Bhāmatī*), attempted to reconcile Sureśvara's position which that of Maṇḍana. Vācaspati contended that *avidyā* has the *jīva* as its locus and is indeterminable. *Brahman*, will remain pure and unsullied by *avidyā* and thereby non-duality will remain.[4] In contradistinction to Vācaspati, Prakāśātman refuted such a view and held that *Brahman* itself is the locus and content of *avidyā*.[5]

Thus, the dialectics grew and an alive and flourishing tradition developed. But it should always be kept in mind that these differences are not irreconcilable within the framework of Advaita and therefore Advaita is not a house divided against itself.

VII.ii KEY-CONCEPT

Ignorance (*avidyā*) is the key-concept of Advaita. It is the device wherein the Advaitin explains how the One, non-dual *Brahman/Ātman* appears as multitudenous. It is by means of this concept that

---

[4]See Preceptors of Advaita, p. 106. *Nāvidyā brahmāśrayā, kintu jīve, sā tu anirvacanīya ityuktam tena nityaśuddham brahma.*

[5]Ibid., p. 107. *Na tāvadajñānam āśraya-viṣaya-bhedāpeksam, kintu ekasminneva vastuni āśrayatvam āvaraṇam cheti krityadvaya sampādayati.*

Advaita delineates its epistemology, metaphysics, and practical teachings. For instance, epistemology presupposes a subject-object duality. Metaphysics must account for the problem of the One and the many; the seeming plurality of the universe; Reality with form and Reality without form; the difference between the individual soul and the Absolute. Practical teachings must explain bondage and liberation; ethics; aesthetics; and values; as well as the disciplines needed for obtaining release. All of this is intelligible and becomes meaningful only in the light of *avidyā* - according to Advaita.

VII.iii. NATURE OF AVIDYĀ

According to Advaita, *avidyā* has six aspects:

1 - It is beginningless (*anadi*);
2 - It can be terminated by knowledge (*jñāna-nivartya*);
3 - It is a positive entity (*bhāva-rūpa*);
4 - Its ontological status is neither real nor unreal (*anirvacanīya*);
5 - It has the two powers of prior concealment (*avaraṇa*) and subsequent denial (*vikṣepa*);
6 - Its locus is either *Brahman/Ātman* or the *jīva*.

VII.iv. LOCUS OF AVIDYĀ - I

Śaṅkara said, "*Avidyā* is *paramesvaraśraya*, that is, it depends upon *Brahman*. And in it (*avidyā*) the individuals souls (*jīva*) having lost their identity with *Brahman*, rest."[6] As we have noted, all Advaitins subscribed to the doctrine that *Brahman* is attributeless, undifferentiated, non-dual and that the universe of multiplicity appears due to ignorance. However, the question arises, 'where is the locus of *avidyā*? If *Brahman* is really *nirguṇa* and *nirviśeṣa*, then there seems to be no place for *avidyā* within it.

Avidyā implies some entity to whom it belongs and some object to which it refers - at least from an empirical point of view. The disagreement comes over the locus of *avidyā* - for all Advaitins posit that *Brahman* is its content. This is obvious because the nature of *avidyā* is to conceal and concealment is possible only with reference to a self-luminous entity. As everything except *Brahman* is inert and insentient, nothing but *Brahman* possesses the capability of necessity for being concealed.

All Advaitins subscribe to the position that *Brahman*, which is *nirguṇa* and *nirviśeṣa*, because of a defect (*doṣa*) called ignorance (*avidyā/māyā*), has the entire universe super-imposed. The Bhāmatī school, first expounded by Maṇḍana, says that the *jīva* is the locus of *avidyā*. Sureśvara subjects this position to a number of objections.

In the *sambandha* to chapter three of the *Naiṣkarmyasiddhi*, Sureśvara gives four reasons why the *jīva* cannot be the locus of *avidyā*.

---

[6] *Brahmasūtrabhāṣya* I.4.3; also see: *Bṛhadāraṇyaka Upaniṣad Bhāṣya* III.viii.12; *Bhagavadgītābhāṣya* XIII.2.

1 - One objection is that it involves the fallacy of reciprocal dependence (*anyonyāśraya* or *petitio principia*). Sureśvara states that it is fallacious to argue that the *jīva* is the result of *avidyā* and, at the same time, *avidyā* has to depend upon the *jīva* as its locus. It is well known that the effect (*jīva*) cannot be earlier in time that its cause (*avidyā*). It is also well known that a locus has nature different from that which it supports. Otherwise, there cannot be the relation of supporter and supported (*ādhāra/adheya*).

(To be fair to the Bhāmatī school, they replied to this objection in two ways. First, it is pointed out that *avidyā* cannot be analysed in a logical, consistent, cogent manner. If this could be done, then *avidyā* would no longer be *avidyā* (*anirvacanīya*)! What holds true for the things of the world is not, and need not be true of *avidyā*. Objects of the world must necessarily follow a causal sequence such that the effect can never be the cause of its cause. And again, no cause which has not come into existence, can produce an effect. However, the space-time-causal sequence does not hold good when applied to *avidyā*. As Maṇḍana remarked, "In *avidyā/māyā* there is nothing which is inconsistent, improbable, illegitimate. If it conveys what is consistent and congruous, it ceases to be *māyā*."[7]

The second way in which Maṇḍana refutes the critics objection is in showing that because both *avidyā* and the *jīva* are beginningless (*anādi*), there is

---

[7] *Brahmasiddhi* Part I, p. 10.

no fallacy of mutual dependence. One does not follow the other in time. He employs an analogy of the seed and sprout series to elucidate the idea that there is no chronological priority for either member of the series. As well, one may ask, 'what came first, the chicken or the egg?' We know that there are chickens, eggs, seeds, sprouts, *avidyā, jīvas,* and to ask which came first is meaningless and irrelevant. *Anādiraprayojana ca avidyā-avidyā* is beginningless and purposeless and thus all questions as to how, why, when, and wherefore do not pertain to it.

Madhusūdana Saraswatī, in his *Advaitasiddhi,* defends the view that the *jīva,* as the locus of *avidyā,* does not involve mutual dependence. He asks, 'If mutual dependence is involved, is it in respect to origin (*utpatti*) or knowledge (*jñapti*) or existence (*sthiti*)?' All three possibilities are untenable. There is no mutual dependence in respect of origin, for, both *avidyā* and the *jīva* are beginningless. Nor is there mutual dependence in respect of their knowledge. *Avidyā* is made known by consciousness (*caitanya*) while the *jīva-caitanya* is self-luminous and self-revealed. Thus it does not require the knowledge of *avidyā* to be known and there is no mutual dependence involved. Lastly, though *avidyā* is dependent on the *jīva-caitanya,* the *jīva-caitanya* does not rest on *avidyā.* Thus, there is no mutual dependence. Nor can we say that one cannot be conceived of without the other, for, though the existence of *avidyā* cannot be thought of apart from the existence of *caitanya,* the *jīva-caitanya* can be thought of apart from the existence of *avidyā.*

In reply, Sarvajñātman of the Vivaraṇa school, points out that *avidyā* presupposes the appearance of the *jīva* and hence cannot be its locus.[8] Even if it is accepted that both the *jīva* and *avidyā* are beginningless, still, this distinction can only be made from the perspective of multiplicity. The idea of a *jīva* does not arise if one has realized *Brahman*. Thus, it follows that the *jīva* derives its existence from *avidyā* - even if *avidyā* does not necessarily require the notion of the *jīva* for its own existence. This relation is not one of cause and effect. To put it in philosophical jargon, it is a mode of the pervaded and the pervader.

Sarvajñātman puts forth two further counter-replies to the Bhāmatī school's position which involve: 1) the fact that the *jīva* is what is technically called a blend of *Brahman* and the internal organ. The consequences of this involve rendering *avidyā* as residing in itself - which is absurd and impossible. 2) an analysis of the deep sleep state which demonstrates that *avidyā* can be experienced even in the absence of the *jīva*.[9]

2 - The second objection raised by Sureśvara is that the *jīva* is an embodiment of ignorance (*ajñāna-svarūpa*). How can ignorance be located in ignorance?

3 - Sureśvara continues, 'suppose for the sake of argument that *avidyā* is located in the *jīva*', even

---

[8] *Saṁkṣepaśārīraka* II.209.

[9] Ibid.

then, what does this accomplish, what can *avidyā* do being located in the *jīva*? It can't do anything over and above what it already does, i.e., its work is concealment (*avaraṇa*), yet it can't do this over and above its locus.

4 - Finally, the *jīva* has no possibility of obtaining knowledge. Ignorance must be in place where it is doing its work of concealing knowledge. That is its legitimate work. And knowledge must be able to arise from *avidyā's* destruction. But if *avidyā* is located in the *jīva*, then knowledge can never arise and liberation will be rendered impossible (as well as the *śruti* rendered useless).

VII.v. LOCUS OF AVIDYĀ - 2

Thus, Sureśvara holds that *Brahman/Ātman* is the locus of *avidyā*, even as darkness is in the house which it conceals. He says,

> Hence, we conclude, as the only remaining alternative, that it is the Self alone which is both the locus (*aśraya*) of and the object (*viṣaya*) concelaed by ignorance.[10]

However, this position is not without its critics. The first and most logical objection to Sureśvara's position is: *Brahman* is of the nature of self-luminous knowledge which is naturally opposed to

---

[10] *Naiṣkarmyasiddhi, sambandha* to chapter III.

avidyā which is of the nature of darkness. Thus, *Brahman* cannot be the locus of *avidyā*.

Vivaraṇa adherents reply to this objection by saying that their true position has been misrepresented. They make a distinction between *Brahman*-knowledge (*svarūpa-jñāna*) and mental cognitions (*vṛtti-jñāna*). *Avidyā*, which is the potency of *Brahman*, is the cause of both valid and erroneous cognitions (which are but *vṛttis* of the mind). Now the bottom line is that it is only *vṛtti-jñāna* which is opposed to *avidyā* and not *svarūpa-jñāna*. *Brahman* is of the nature of knowledge and reveals everything, including *avidyā*. We observed earlier that there is no conflict between the revealer and the revealed.

The second objection to the Vivaraṇa position states that if *Brahman/Ātman* is the locus of *avidyā*, then it cannot remove *avidyā*. This is due to the above stated position which claims that *Brahman/Ātman* is not opposed to *avidyā* if it is its locus.

However, Sureśvara never said that *Brahman/Ātman* removes *avidyā*. It is *vṛtti-jñāna* which removes *avidyā* and not *svarūpa-jñāna*. *Vṛtti-jñāna* applies to the empirical or relative level. As a valid/means of knowledge (*pramāṇa*), it involves the duality of a knower, what is known, and the process thereby. This entire operation presupposes *avidyā*. Even this very objection presupposes *avidyā*.

If one asks why *Brahman*-knowledge as-it-is cannot remove *avidyā* when *Brahman*-knowledge passed through a mental mode can, an analogy is given. The light of the sun, when passed through a magnifying glass, can burn a combustible substance while that same light, by itself, cannot.

A third objection contends that *Brahman/Ātman* is partless (*nirviśeṣa*). This has the consequence of rendering *Brahman/Ātman* relationless, which, *ipso facto*, means that it cannot be a locus of anything let alone *avidyā*. In fact, there is nothing else for It to be a locus for!

In response, the Advaitin maintains that an individual must have knowledge of *avidyā*, and thereby a universe of multiplicity, in order to say that it is other than *Brahman*. If one does not know that the universe exists, one cannot label it true or false. As well, one must know the real nature of *Brahman* in order to say that the universe if false. It is incumbent that ignorance be removed before one knows the real nature of *Brahman*. Thus, the critic is presupposing that *avidyā* is real and locates somewhere. If an individual speaks of *avidyā*, then *Brahman/Ātman* must be its locus, BUT, really there is no *avidyā* at all. Relations pertain only at the relative level - not at the Absolute level.

Thus, according to Sureśvara, *Brahman/Ātman* must be the locus and content of *avidyā*. All that is not *Brahman/Ātman* is of the nature of ignorance and it does not make any sense to say that ignorance is located in what is of the nature of ignorance. If that were the case, there would be no scope for ignorance's work of concealment in respect to the world of multiplicity. As well, what owes its very existence to *avidyā*, cannot be its support as well. Neither can the locus of *avidyā* have a nature dependent upon, nor similar to, *avidyā* - or vice versa.

Avidyā is unreal, from any Advaitin's perspective. Thus, in truth, it does not need a real residence anywhere. It is only from an ignorant individual's perspective that the question arises at all. This point cannot be stressed enough.

Transliteration of

The Naiṣkarmyasiddhi

prathamo 'dhyāyaḥ

ābrahmastambaparyantaiḥ sarvaprāṇibhiḥ sarvaprakāra syāpi duḥkhasya svarasata eva jihāsitatvāt, tannivṛttyarthā pravṛttirasti svarasata eva. duḥkhasya ca dehopādānaikahetutvād, dehasya ca pūrvopacitadharmādharmamūlatvādanucchittiḥ. tayośca vihitapratiṣiddhakarmamūlatvād anivṛttiḥ. karmaṇaśca rāgadveṣāpadatvad rāgadveṣayośca śobhanāśobhanādhyāsanibandhanatvād, adhyāsasya cāvicāritasiddhadvaitavastu nimittatvād, dvaitasya ca śuktikārajatādivat sarvasyāpi svataḥ-siddhādvitīyātmānavabodhamātropādānatvādavyāvṛttiḥ. ataḥ sarvānarthaheturātmānavabodha eva. sukhasya cānāgamāpāyino 'paratantrasyātmasvabhāvatvāt tasyānavabodhaḥ pidhānam. atas tasyātyantocchittāvaśeṣapuruṣārthaparisamāptiḥ. ajñānanivṛtteśca samyagjñānasvarūpalābhamātrahetutvāt tadupādānam. aśeṣānārthahetvātmānavabodhaviṣayasya cānāgamikapratyakṣādilaukikapramāṇāviṣayatvāt vedāntāgamavākyādeva samyagjñānam. ato śeṣavedāntasārasaṃgrahaprakaraṇamidam ārabhyate. tatrābhilaṣitārthapracayāya prakaraṇārthasaṃsūtraṇāya cāyamādyaḥ ślokaḥ.

khānilāgnyabdharitryantaṃ srakphaṇīvodgataṃ yataḥ
dvāntacchide namastasmai haraye buddhisākṣiṇe (1)

svasaṃpradāyasya coditapramāṇapūrvakatvajñāpanāya viśiṣṭaguṇasaṃbandhasaṃkīrtanapūrvikā gurornamaskārakriyā

alabdhvātiśayaṃ yasmād vyāvṛttāstamabādayaḥ
garīyase namastasmā avidyāgranthibhedine (2)

namaskāranimittasvāśayāviṣkaraṇārthaḥ

vedāntodarasaṃgūḍhaṃ saṃsārotsāri vastugam
jñānam vyākṛtamapyanyairvakṣye gurvanuśikṣayā (3)

kiṃ viṣayaṃ prakaraṇamiti cet, tadupanyāsaḥ

yatsiddhāvidamaḥ siddhir yadasiddhau na kiṃcana
pratyagdharmaikaniṣṭhasya yāthātmyaṃ vakṣyate
sphuṭam (4)

vivakṣitaprakaraṇārthaprarocanāyā anuktaduruk-
tāprāmāṇya kāraṇaśaṅkāvyudāsena svaguroḥ
prāmāṇyopavarṇanam

gurūkto vedarāddhāntastatra no vacmy aśaktitaḥ
sahasrakiraṇavyāpte khadyotaḥ kiṃ prakāśayet (5)

guruṇaiva vedārthasya parisamāpitatvat prakaranoktau
khyātyādyaprāmāṇyakāraṇāśaṅketi cet, tadvyudāsārtham
āha

na khyātilābhapūjārthaṃ grantho'smābhir udīryate
svabodhapariśuddhyarthaṃ brahmavinnikaṣāśmasu (6)

anarthānarthahetupuruṣārthataddhetuprakaraṇārthasaṃ-
grahajñāpanāyopanyāsaḥ

aikātmyāpratipattir yā svātmānubhavasaṃśraya
sā'vidyā saṃsṛterbījaṃ tannāśo muktirātmanaḥ (7)

puruṣārthahetoravaśiṣṭatvāt tadabhivyāhārah

vedāvasānavākyotthasamyagjñānaśuśukṣaṇiḥ
dandahītyātmano mohaṃ na karmāpratikūlataḥ (8)

pratijñātārthasaṃśuddhyarthaṃpūrvapakṣoktiḥ. tatra jñānamabhyupagamya tāvadupanyāsaḥ

mukteḥ kriyābhiḥ siddhatvājjñānam tatra karoti kim
kathaṃ chṛṇu tatsarvaṃ praṇidhyāya mano yathā (9)

akurvataḥ kriyāḥ kāmyā niṣiddhāstyajatastathā
nityanaimittikāṃ karma vidhivac cānutiṣṭhataḥ (10)

kim ato bhavati?

kāmyakarmaphalaṃ tasmāddevādimaṃ na ḍhaukate
niṣiddhasya nirastatvānnārakīṃ naity adhojanim (11)

dehārambhakayośca dharmādharmayorjñānimā saha karmiṇaḥ samānau codyaparihārau

vartamānam idaṃ yābhyāṃ sariram sukhaduḥkhadam
ārabdhaṃpuṇyapāpābhyāṃ bhogād eva tayoḥ kṣayaḥ (12)

kāmyapratiśiddhakarmaphalatvāt saṃsārasya tannirāsenaivāśeṣānarthanirāsasya siddhatvāt kiṃ nityānuṣṭhāneneti cet, tan na. tadakaraṇādapyanarthaprasakteḥ

nityānuṣṭhānataś cainam pratyavāyo na saṃspṛśet
anādṛtyātmavijñānamatah karmāṇi saṃśrayet (13)

abhyupetyaivam ucyate na tu yathāvasthitātmavastu viṣayam jñānam asti, tatpratipādakapramāṇābhāvāt

yāvantyaś ceha vidyante śrutayas smṛtibhis saha
vidadhaty uruyatnena karmāto bhūrisādhanam (14)

syāt pramāṇāsaṃbhavo bhavad-aparādhād iti cet, tan na. yataḥ

yatnato vīkṣamāṇo'pi vidhiṁ jñānasya na kvacit
śrutau smṛtau vā paśyāmi viśvāso nānyato'sti naḥ (15)

syāt pravṛttirantareṇāpi vidhiṃ lokavad iti cet, tan na. yataḥ

antareṇa vidhiṃ mohād yah kuryāt sāmparāyikam
na tat syād upakārāya bhasmanīva hutaṃ haviḥ (16)

abhyupagata prāmāṇya vedartha vij jaiminy anuśāsanac ca

"āmnāyasya kriyārthatvād ānarthakyam" ito'nyathā
iti sāṭopam āhoccair vedavij jaiminiḥ svayam (17)

mantravarṇāc ca

"kurvann eveha karmāṇi jijiviṣec chataṃ samāḥ"
iti mantro'pi niśśeṣam karmāṇy āyur avāṣrjat (18)

jñāninaś ca vastuni vākya pramāṇyābhyupagamād, vākyasya ca kriyāpadapradhānatvāt tataś cābhipreta-jñānābhāvaḥ

virahayya kriyāṃ naiva saṃhanyante padānyapi
na samasty apadaṃ vākyaṃ yat syāj jñānavidhāyakam (19)

jñānābhyupagame'pi na doṣaḥ. yataḥ

karmaṇo'ṅgāṅgibhāvena svapradhānatayā'thavā
saṃbandhasyeha saṃsiddher jñāne saty apy adoṣataḥ (20)

yasmāj jñānābhyupagamānabhyupagame'pi na jñānān muktiḥ

ataḥ sarvāśramāṇāṃ hi vāṅ manaḥ kāyakarmabhiḥ
svanuṣṭhitair yathā śakti muktiḥ syān nānyasādhanāt (21)

asadarthapralāpo'yam iti dūṣaṇasaṃbhāvanāyāh a

iti hṛṣṭadhiyāṃ vācaḥ svaprajñādhmātacetasām
ghuṣyante yajñaśālāsu dhūmānaddhadhiyāṃ kila (22)

dūṣaṇopakramāvadhi jñāpanāyāh a

atrābhidadhmahe doṣān kramaśo nyāyabṛṃhitaiḥ
vacobhiḥ pūrvpakṭoti ghātibhir nātisaṃbhramāt (23)

caturvidhasyāpi karmakāryasya muktāv asaṃbhavān na mukteḥ karmakāryatvam

ajñānahānamātratvān mukteḥ karma na sādhanam
karmāpamārṣṭi nājñānaṃ tamasīvotthitaṃ tamaḥ (24)

karmakāryatvābhyupagame'pi doṣa eva

ekena vā bhaven muktir yadi vā sarvakarmabhiḥ
pratyekaṃ cedvṛthānyāni sarvebhyo'pyekakarmatā (25)

sarvaprakārasyāpi karmaṇa utpattita eva viśiṣṭasādhyābhisaṃbandhān na pāriśeṣyanyāyasiddhiḥ

duritakṣapaṇārthatvān na nityaṃ syād vimuktaye
svargādiphala saṃbandhāt kāmyaṃ karma tathaiva na (26)

pramāṇāsaṃbhavāc ca

sādhyasādhanabhāvo'yaṃ vacanāt pāralaukikaḥ
nāśrauṣaṃ mokṣadaṃ karma śruter vaktrāt kathaṃcana (27)

abhyupagatābhyupagamāc ca śvaśrūnirgacchoktivad bhavato niṣprayojanaḥ pralāpaḥ

niṣiddha kāmyayos tyāgas tvayāpiṣṭo yathā mayā
nityasyāphalavattvāc ca na mokṣaḥ karmasādanaḥ (28)

evaṃ tāvat "mukteḥ kriyābhiḥ siddhatvāt" iti nirasto'yaṃ pakṣaḥ. athādhunā sarvakarmapravṛttihetunirūpaṇena yathāvasthitātmavastuviśayakevalajñānamātrād eva sakalasaṃsārānarthanivṛttir itīmaṃ pakṣaṃ draḍhayitukāma āha. iha cedaṃ parīkṣyate. kiṃ yathā pratiṣiddheṣu yādṛcchikeṣu ca karmasu svābhāvikasvāśayotthanimittavāśad eva "idam hitam, idam ahitam" iti viśeṣān parikalpya mṛgatṛṣṇikodaka-pipāsur iva laukikapramāṇaprasiddhāny eva sādhanāny upādāya hitaprāptaye-'hitanirāsāya ca svayameva pra-vartate nivartate ca, tathaivādṛṣṭārtheṣu kāmyeṣu nityeṣu ca karmasu. kiṃ vānyad eva tatra pravṛttinivṛttinimittam? iti. kiṃ cāto yady evaṃ?, śṛṇu, yadi tavād yathāvasthitavastu samyagjñānaṃ pramāṇabhūtam laukikam āgamikaṃ vā pra-vṛttinimittam iti niścīyate, nivṛttiśastraṃ ca nābhyupagamyate, tadā hatāḥ karmatyāgino, bhrāntivijñāna-mātrāvaṣṭambhād, alaukikapramāṇopattakarmānuṣṭhāna-tyāgitvāc ca. atha mṛgatṛṣṇikodakapipāsupravṛttinimitta vadayathāvastu bhrāntivijñānam eva sarvapravṛttinimittam tadā varddhāmahe vayam hatāḥ stha yūyam iti

hitam samprepsatām mohād ahitam ca jihāsatām
upāyān prāptihānārthān śāstram bhāsayate'rkavat (29)

evam tāvat pratyakṣānumānāgamapramāṇāvaṣṭambhād-ātmano niratiśayasukhahitāvyatirekasiddher, ahitasya ca ṣaṣṭhagocaravat svata evānabhisamabandhād, evamsvābhāvyātmānavabodhamātrād eva "hitam me syād ahitam me mā bhūd" iti mithyājñānam tūṣaraśuktikānavabodhottha-mithyājñānavat pravṛttinimittamiti nirdhāritam. śāstram ca na padārthaśaktyādhānakṛditi. athaitasyaivottaratra prapañca ārabhyate

na parīnsīm jihāsām vā puṃsāḥ śāstram karoti hi
nije eva tu te yasmāt paśvādāvapi darśanāt (30)

uktam tāvadanavabuddhavastuyāthātmya eva vidhi-pratiṣedhaśāstresv adhikriyata iti. athādhunā viṣaya-svābhāvanurodhena pravṛttyasambhavam vaktukāma āha

lipsate'jñānato'labdham kaṇthe cāmikaram yathā
varjitam ca svato bhrāntyā chāyāyāmātmano yathā
bhayān mohāvanaddhātmā rakṣaḥ parijihirṣati
yac cāparihṛtam vastu tathā'labdham ca lipsate (31 & 32)

tatraiteṣu caturṣu viṣayeṣu prāptaye parihārāya ca vibhajya nyāyaḥ pradarśyate

prāptavyaparihāryeṣu jñātvopāyāñ śruteḥ pṛthak
kṛtvātha prāpnuyāt prāpyam tathā'niṣṭam jahāty api (33)

athāvaśiṣṭayoḥ svabhāvata eva

varjitāvāptayor bodhādd hānaprāpti na karmaṇā
mohamātrāntarāyatvāt kriyayā te na sidhyataḥ (34)

kasmāt punarātmavastuyāthātmyāvabodhamātrād evābhilaṣitaniratiśayasukhāvāptiniśśeṣaduḥkha-nivṛtti bhavato na tu karmaṇeti? ucyate

karmājñānasamutthatvān nālaṃ mohāpanuttaye
samyagjñānaṃ virodhyaśya tāmisrasyāṃśumān iva (35)

nany ātmajñānam apy avidyopādānam. na hi śāstraśiṣyācāryādy anupādāyātmajñānam ātmānaṃ labhata iti. naiṣa doṣaḥ. yata ātmajñānam hi svatassiddhaparamārthātmavastusvarūpamātrāśrayād evāvidyātadutpannakārakagrāmapradhvaṃsi svātmotpattāv eva śāstrady apekṣate, notpannamavidyānivṛttau. karma punaḥ svātmotpattāv utpannaṃ ca. na hi kriyā kārakanisspṛhā kalpakoṭivyavahitaphaladānāya svātmānaṃ bibharti sādhyamānamātrarūpatvāt tasyāḥ. na ca kriyātmajñānavat svātmapratilambhakāla eva svargādi-phalena kartāraṃ saṃbadhnāti. ātmajñānaṃ punaḥ puruṣārthasiddhau notpadyamānasvarūpavyatirekeṇānyad-rūpāntaraṃ sādhanāntaraṃ vāpekṣate. kuta etat? yataḥ.

balavaddhi pramāṇotthaṃ samyagjñānaṃ na bādhyate
ākāṅkṣate na cāpy anyad bādhanaṃ prati sādhanam (36)

svapakṣasya hetvavaṣṭambhena samarthitatvān nirāśaṅkam-upasaṃhriyate

taśmād duḥkhodadher hetor ajñānasyāpanuttaye
samyagjñānaṃ sup aryāptaṃ kriyā cen noktahetutaḥ (37)

nanu balavad api samyagjñānaṃ sad apramāṇotthenāsamyagjñānena bādhyamānam upalabhāmahe yata utpannaparamārthabodhasyāpi kartṛtvabhoktṛtvarāgadveṣādyanavabodhotthapratyayā āvirbhavanti. na hy abādhite samyagjñāne tadviruddhānāṃ pratyayānāṃ saṃbhavo'sti. naitadevam. kutaḥ?

bādhitatvād avidyāyā vidyām sā naiva bādhate
tadvāsanā nimittatvaṃ yānti vidyāsmṛter dhruvam (38)

"karmājñānasamutthatvāt" ity ukto hetustasya ca samarthanaā pūrvam evābhihitaṃ "hitaṃ samprepsatām" ity ādinā. tadabhyuccayārtham avidyānvayena ca saṃsārānvayitvaṃ pradarśayiṣyāmīty ata āh a

brāhmaṇy ādyātmake dehe lātvā nātmeti bhāvanām
śruteḥ kiṅkaratām eti vāṅ manaḥ kāyakarmasu (39)

yasmāt karmājñānasamutthameva tasmāt tadvyāvṛttau nivartata ity ucyate

dagdhākhilādhikāraś ced brahmajñānāgnina muniḥ
vartamānaḥ śruter mūrdhni naiva syād vedakiṅkaraḥ (40)

athetaro ghanatarāvidyāpaṭalasaṃvitāntaḥkaraṇo'ṅgikṛtakartṛtvādyaśeṣakarmādhikārakāraṇo vidhipratiṣedhacodanāsaṃdaṃśopadaṣṭaḥ karmasu pravartamānaḥ

śubhaiḥ prāpnoti devatvaṃ niṣiddhair nārakīṃ gatim
ubhābhyāṃpuṇyapāpābhyāṃ mānuṣyaṃ labhate'vaśaḥ (41)

ābrahmastambaparyante ghore duḥkhodadhau ghaṭīyantravad ārohāvarohanyāyenādhamamadhyamottamasukhaduḥkhamohavidyuccapalasaṃpātadāyinīrvicitrayoniścaṇḍotpiñjalakaśvasanavegābhihatāmbhodhimadhyavartiśuṣkālābuvat śubhāśubhavyāmiśrakarmavāyusamīritaḥ

evam caṅkramyamāṇo'yamavidyākāmakarmabhiḥ
pāsito jāyate kāmī mriyate cāsukhāvṛtah (42)

yathokte'rtha ādaravidhānāya pramāṇopanyāsaḥ

śrutiś cemaṃ jagādārthaṃ kāmasya vinivṛttaye
tanmūlā saṃsṛtir yasmāt tannāśo'jñānahānataḥ (43)

kā tv asau śrutir iti cet

"yadā sarve pramucyanta" "iti nu" iti ca vājinaḥ
kāmabandhanam evedaṃ vyāso'py āha pade pade (44)

eṣa saṃsārapanthā vyākhyātaḥ. athedānīṃ tadvyāvṛttaye karmāṇy ārādupakārakatvena yathā mokṣahetutāṃ pratipadyante, tathābhidhīyate

tasyaivaṃduḥkhataptasya kathaṃcit puṇyaśīlanāt
nityehākṣālitadhiyo vairāgyaṃ jāyate hṛdi (45)

kīdṛg vairāgyamutpadyata iti? ucyate

narakād bhīr yathāsyābhūt tathā kāmyaphalād api
yathārthadarśanāt tasmān nityaṃ karma cikīrṣati (46)

evaṃ nityanaimittikakarmānuṣṭhānena
śudhyamānaṃ tu taccittam īśvarārpitakarmabhiḥ

vairāgyaṃ brahmālokadau vyanaktyatha sunirmalam (47)

yasmād rajastamomalopasaṃsṛṣṭa meva cittaṃ kāmabaḍiśenakṛṣya viṣayadurantasūnāsthāneṣu nikṣipyate, tasmānnityanaimittikakarmānuṣṭhānaparimārjanenāpaviddharajastamo-malaṃ prasannam ānakulam, saṃmārjitasphaṭikaśilākalpaṃ, bāhyaviṣayahetukena ca rāgadveṣātmakenātigrahabādi-śenānākṛṣyamāṇaṃ vidhūtāśeṣakalmaṣaṃ pratyammātra-pravaṇaṃ cittadarpaṇamavatiṣṭhate. ata idam abhidhīyate

vyutthitāśeṣakāmebhyo yadā dhir avatiṣṭhate
tadaiva pratyagātmānaṃ svayam evāviviksati (48)

ataḥ param avasitādhikārāṇi karmāṇi pratyakpravaṇatvasūnau kṛtasaṃprattikāni caritārthāni santi

pratyakpravaṇatāṃ buddheḥ karmāṇy utpādya śuddhitaḥ
kṛtārthānyastamāyānti prāvṛḍante ghanā iva (49)

yato nityakarmānuṣṭhānasyaiṣa mahimā

tasmān mumukṣubhiḥ kāryam ātmajñānābhilāṣibhiḥ
nityaṁ naimittikaṁ karma sadaivātmaviśuddhaye (50)

yathokte'rthe sarvajñavacanam pramāṇam

"ārurukṣor muner yogaṃ karma kāraṇam ucyate
yogārūḍhasya tasyaiva śama" eveti ca smṛtiḥ (51)

nityakarmānuṣṭhānād dharmotpattir, dharmotpatteḥ pāpahānis, tataś cittaśuddhis tataḥ saṃsārayāthātmyāvabodhas, tato vairāgyam, tato mumukṣutvaṃ, tatas tadupāyaparyeṣaṇaṃ, tataḥ sarvakarmatatsādhanasaṃnyāsas, tato yogābhyāsas, tataś cittasya pratyakpravaṇatā, tatas tattvamasyādivākyārthaparijñānaṃ, tato 'vidyocchedas, tataś ca svātmany evāvasthānaṃ "brahmaiva san brahmāpyeti" "vimuktaś ca vimucyate" iti

pāramparyeṇa karmaivaṃ syād avidyānivṛttaye
jñānavan nāvirodhitvāt karmāvidyāṃ nirasyati (52)

na ca karmaṇaḥ kāryam aṇy api muktau saṃbhāvyate. nāpi muktau yat saṃbhavati tat karmāpekṣate. tad ucyate.

utpādyam āpyaṃ saṃskāryaṃ vikāryaṃ ca kriyāphalam
naivaṃ muktir yatas tasmāt karma tasyā na sādhanam (53)

evaṃ tāvat kevalaṃ karma sākṣād avidyāpanuttaye na paryāptamiti prapañcitam. muktau ca mumukṣujñānatadviṣayasvābhāvyānurodhena sarvaprakārasyāpi karmaṇo'sam bhava ukto "hitaṃ saṃprepsatām" ity ādinā. yādṛśaścārādupakārakatvena jñānotpattau karmaṇāṃ samuccayaḥ saṃbhavati, tathā pratipāditam. avidyocchittau tu labdhātmasvabhāvasyātmajñānasyaivāsādhāraṇaṃ sādhakatamatvaṃ, nānyasya pradhānabhātasya guṇabhūtasya cetyetadadhunocyate. tatra jñānam guṇabhūtaṃ tāv-adahetur ity etad āha

saṃnipatya na ca jñānaṃ karmājñānaṃ nirasyati
sādhyasādhanabhāvatvādekakālānavasthiteḥ (54)

samapradhānayor apy asaṃbhava eva

bādhyabādhakabhāvāc ca pañcāsyoraṇayor iva
ekadeśānavasthānān na samuccayatā tayoḥ (55)

kuto bādhyabādhakabhāvaḥ? yasmāt

ayathāvastvavidyā syād vidyā tasyā virodhinī
samuccayas tayor evaṃ raviśārvarayor iva (56)

tasmād akārakabrahmātmani parisamāptāvabodhasyāśeṣa-karmacodanānām acodyasvābhāvyāt kuṇṭhatā. kathaṃ tat? abhidhīyate

bṛhaspatisave yadvat kṣattriyo na pravartate
brāhmaṇatvādyahammānī vipro vā kṣattrakarmaṇi (57)

yathāyaṃ dṛṣṭānta evaṃ dārṣṭāntiko'pity etad āha

videho vītasaṃdeho neti netyavaśeṣitaḥ
dehādyanātmadṛk tadvat tatkriyaṃ vikṣate'pi na (58)

tasyārthasyāviṣkaraṇārtham udāharaṇam

mṛtsnebhake yathebhatvaṃ śiśur adhyasya valgati
adhyasyātmani dehādin mūḍhas tadvad vicesṭate (59)

na ca vayaṃ jñānakarmaṇoḥ sarvatraiva samuccayaṃ pratyācakṣmahe. yatra prayojyaprayojakabhāvo jñāna-karmaṇos, tatra nāsmatpitrāpi śakyate nivārayitum. tatra vibhāgapradarśanayodāharaṇaṃ pradarśyate

sthāṇuṃ coradhiyālāya bhito yadvat palāyate
buddhyādibhis tathātmānaṃ bhrānto'dhyāropya ceṣṭate (60)

evaṃ yatra-yatra jñānakarmaṇoḥ prayojyaprayojakabhāvas, tatra sarvatrāyaṃ nyāyaḥ. yatra tu na samakālaṃ nāpi krameṇopapadyate samuccayaḥ, sa viṣaya ucyate

sthāṇoh satattvavijñānaṃ yathā nāṇgam palāyane
ātmanas tattvavijñānaṃ tadvan nāṅgaṃ kriyāvidhau (61)

yasmādguṇasyaitat svābhāvyam

yadd hi yasyānurodhena svabhāvam anuvartate
tat tasya guṇabhūtaṃ syān na pradhānādguṇo yataḥ (62)

yasmāt

karmaprakaraṇākāṅkṣi jñānaṃ karmaguṇo bhavet
yadd hi prakaraṇe yasya tattadṅngaṃ pracakṣate (63)

svarūpalābhamātreṇa yattvavidyāṃ nihanti naḥ
na tad aṅgaṃ pradhānaṃ vā jñānaṃ syāt karmaṇaḥ kvacit
(64)

samuccayapakṣavādināpy avaśyam etad abhyupagantavyam. yasmāt

ajñānam anirākurvaj jñānameva na sidhyati
vipannakārakagrāmaṃ jñānam karma na ḍhaukate (65)

idaṃ cāparaṃ kāraṇaṃ jñānakarmaṇoḥ samuccayanibarhi

hetusvarūpakāryāṇi prakāśatamasor iva
virodhīni tato nāsti sāṅgatyaṃ jñānakarmaṇoḥ (66)

evamupasaṃhṛtekecit sva-saṃpradāyabalāvaṣṭambhād āhur, yadetadvedānta-vākyād "ahaṃ brahmeti" vijñānaṃ samutpadyate, tannaiva svotpattimātreṇājñānaṃ nirasyati. kiṃ tarhi? ahanyahani drāghīyasā kālenopāsīnasya sato bhāvanopacayān niśśeṣamajñānamapagacchati, "devo bhūtvā devān apyeti" iti śruteḥ. apare tu bruvate, vedāntavākyajanitam "ahaṃ brahmeti" iti vijñānam saṃsargātmakatvād, ātmavastuyāthātmyāvagāhy eva na bhavati. kiṃ tarhi? etadeva gaṅgāsrotovat satatamabhyasyato'nyad evāvākyārthātmakaṃ vijñānāntaramutpadyate. tad evāśeṣājñānatimirotsāriti, "vijñāya prajñāṃ kurvīta brāhmaṇaḥ" iti śruteriti. asya pakṣadvayasya nivṛttaya idam abhidhīyate.

sakṛtpravṛttyā mṛdnāti kriyā kārakarūpabhṛt
ajñānam āgamajñānaṃ sāṅgatyaṃ nāsty ato'nayoḥ (67)

evaṃ tāvad anānātve brahmaṇi jñānakarmaṇoḥ samuccayo nirākṛtaḥ. athādhunā pakṣāntarābhyupagamenāpi pratyavasthānepūrvavadanāśvāso yathā tathābhidhīyate

anutsāritanānātvaṃ brahma yasyāpi vādinaḥ
taṇmatenāpi dussādhyo jñānakarmasamuccayaḥ (68)

tasya vibhāgoktir dūṣaṇavibhāgaprajñaptaye

brahmātmā vā bhavettasya yadi vānātmarūpakam
ātmānāptir bhaven mohād itarasyāpy anātmanaḥ (69)

tatra yadi tāvad vāstavenaiva vṛttena brahma prāptam ātmasvābhāvyāt, kevalam āsuramohāpidhānamātramevānāpti-nimittaṃ, tasmin pakṣe

mohāpidhānabhaṅgāya naiva karmāṇi kāraṇam
jñānenaiva phalāv āptes tatra karma nirarthakam (70)

anātmarūpake tu brahmaṇi na karma sādhanabhāvaṃ pratipadyate, nāpi jñānaṃ karmasamuccitam asamuccitaṃ vā, yasmād anyasya svata eva sādhakasya brahmaṇo'py-anyatvaṃ svata eva siddham. tatraivam

anyasyānyātmatāprāptau na kvaciddhetusaṃbhavaḥ
tasmin saty api nānaṣṭaḥ parātmānaṃ prapadyate (71)

aparasmiṃs tu pakṣe vidhiḥ

paramātmānukūlena jñānābhyāsena duḥkhinaḥ
dvaitino'pi pramucyeran na parātmavirodhinā (72)

itarasmiṃs tu pakṣe vidher evānavakāśatvam. katham?

samastavyastabhūtasya brahmaṇy evāvatiṣṭhataḥ
brūta karmaṇi ko hetuḥ sarvānanyatvadarśinaḥ (73)

sarvakarmanimittasaṃbhavāsaṃbhavābhyāṃ sarvakarma-saṅkaraś ca prāpnoti. yasmāt

sarvajātyādimattvek'sya nitarāṃ hetvasaṃbhavaḥ
viśeṣaṃ hy anupādāya karma naiva pravartate (74)

syād vidhir adhyātmābhimānād iti cen, naivam. yasmāt

na cādhyātmābhimano'pi viduṣo'sty āsuratvataḥ
viduṣo'py āsuraś cet syān niṣphalaṃ brahmadarśanam (75)

ajñānakāryatvān na samakālaṃ nāpi krameṇa jñānakarmaṇor-vastvavastutantratvāt saṅgatir astīty evam nirākṛto'pi, kāśaṃ kuśaṃ vāvalambyāh a

athādhyātmaṃ punar yāyād āśrito mūḍhatāṃ bhavet
sa karotyeva karmāṇi ko hy ajñaṃ vinivārayet (76)

siddhatvāc ca na sādhyam. yataḥ

sāmānyetararūpābhyāṃ karmātmaivāsya yoginaḥ
niśśvāsocchvāsavat tasmān na niyogam apekṣate (77)

astu tarhi bhinnābhinnātmakaṃ brahma. tathā ca sati jñāna-karmaṇī saṃbhavato bhedābhedaviṣayatvāt tayoḥ. tatra tāvad ayaṃ pakṣa eva na saṃbhavati. kiṃ kāraṇam? na hi bhinno'yam ity abhedabuddhim anirākṛtya bhedabuddhiḥ padārtham āliṅgate. evaṃ hy anabhyupagame bhinnābhinna-padārthayor alaukikatvaṃ prasajyeta. atha niṣpramāṇakam apy āśrīyate, tad apy ubhaya-pakṣābhyupagamād abheda-pakṣe duḥkhi brahma syād ata āha

bhinnābhinnaṃ viśeṣaiś ced duḥkhi syād brahma te dhruvam
aśeṣaduḥkhitā ca syād aho prajñātma vādinām (78)

tasmāt samyag evābhihitaṃ na jñānakarmaṇoḥ samuccaya ity upasaṃhriyate

tamo'ngatvaṃ yathā bhānor agneś śītāṅgatā yathā
vāriṇaś coṣṇatā yadvaj jñānasyaivaṃ kriyāṅgatā (79)

yathoktopapattibalenaiva pūrvapakṣayotsāritatvād, vak-tavyaṃ nāvaśeṣitam ity ataḥ pratipattikarmavat pūrva-pakṣaparihārāya yatkiñcid vaktavyam ity ata idam abhi-dhīyate

"mukteḥ kriyābhiḥ siddhatvāt" ity ādy anucitaṃ bahu
yad abhāṇi tad anyāyyaṃ yathā tadadhunocyate (80)

yo'yaṃ kāmyānāṃ pratiṣiddhānāṃ ca tyāgaḥ pratijñāyate, sā pratijñā tāvan na śakyate'nuṣṭhātum. kiṃ kāraṇam? karmaṇo hi nirvṛttātmano dvābhyāṃ prakārābhyāṃ nivṛttiḥ saṃbhavaty, ārabdhaphalasyopabhogenā, nārabdhaphalasyāśubhaṣya prāyaścittair iti. tṛtīyo'pi tyāgaprakāro'kartrātmāvabodhat, sa tvātmajñānānabhyupagamād bhavatā nābhyupagamyate. tatra yāny anupabhuktaphalāny anārabdhaphalāni, tānīṣvareṇāpi kenacid api na śakyante parityaktum. athārabdhaphalāni tyajyante, tāny api na śakyante tyaktum. kiṃ kāraṇam? anivṛtteḥ. anirvṛttaṃ hi cikīrṣitaṃ karma śakyate tyaktuṃ, pravṛttinivṛttī prati kartuḥ svātantryāt. nirvṛtte tu karmaṇi tadasaṃbhavādduranuṣṭheyaḥ pratijñātārthaḥ. aśakyapratijñānāc ca. na ca śakyate pratijñātuṃ "yāvajjīvaṃ kāmyāni pratiṣiddhāni ca karmāṇi na kariṣyām" iti sunipuṇānām api sūkṣmāparādhadarśanāt. pramāṇābhāvāc ca. na ca pramāṇam asti, mokṣakāmo nityanaimittike karmaṇī kuryāt, kāmyapratiṣiddhe ca varjayed, ārabdhaphale copabhogena kṣapayed iti. ānantyāc ca. na copacitānāṃ karmaṇām iyattāsti, saṃsārasyānāditvāt. na ca kāmyaiḥ pratiṣiddhair vā teṣāṃ nivṛttir asti, śuddhyaśuddhisāmye saty avirodhād ity āha

na kṛtsnakāmyasaṃtyāgo'nantatvāt kartum iṣyate
niṣiddhakarmaṇaśceha vyatītānantajanmasu (81)

syān mataṃ vyatītānantajanmopāttānāṃ karmaṇām

kṣayo nityena teṣāṃ cet prāyaścittair yathainasaḥ
niṣphalatvān na nityena kāmyāder vinivāraṇām (82)

pramāṇābhāvāc ca. katham?

pāpāpanuttaye vākyāt prāyaścittaṃ yathā tathā
gamyate kāmyahānārthaṃ nityaṃ karma na vākyataḥ (83)

athāpi syāt kāmyair eva kāmyānāṃ pūrvajanmopacitānāṃ kṣayo bhaviṣyatīti. tan na. yataḥ

pāpmanāṃ pāpmabhir nāsti yathaiveha nirākriyā
kāmyair api tathaivāstu kāmyānām avirodhataḥ (84)

evaṃ tāvat "mukteḥ kriyābhiḥ siddhatvāt" iti nirākṛtam. athātmajñānasya sadbhāve pramāṇāsaṃbhava uktas tatparihārāyaha

śrutayas smṛtibhis sākam ānantyāt kāminām iha
vidadhaty uruyatnena karmāto bahukāmadam (85)

na ca bāhulyaṃ prāmāṇye kāraṇabhāvaṃ pratipadyate. ata āha

prāmāṇyāya na bāhulyaṃ na hyekatra pramāṇatām
vastuny aṭanti mānāni tv ekatraikasya mānatā (86)

yat tūktaṃ "yatnato vīkṣamāṇo'pi" iti tatrāpi, bhavata evāparādhaḥ. kasmāt? yataḥ

"parīkṣya lokān" ity ādyā ātmajñānavidhāyinīḥ
naiṣkarmyapravaṇās sādhviḥ śrutiḥ kiṃ na śṛṇoṣi tāḥ (87)

nanu "ātmety evopāsīta", "ātmā vā are draṣṭavyaḥ" ityapūrvabidhiśruteḥ puruṣasyātmadarśanakriyāyāṃ niyogo'vasīyata iti. naivam. apuruṣatantratvād vastuyāthātmyajñānasya sakalanārthabījātmanavabodhotsāriṇo muktihetor iti. vidhy abhyupagame'pi nāpūrvavidhir ayam. ata āha

niyamaḥ parisaṅkhyā vā vidhyartho'pi bhaved yataḥ
anātmādarśanenaiva parātmānam upāsmahe (88)

yac coktaṃ "viśāso nānyato'sti naḥ" iti, tad api nidrātura-cetasā tvayā svapnāyamānena pralapitam. kiṃ kāraṇam? na hi vayaṃ pramāṇabalenaikātmyaṃ pratipadyāmaha, aikātmyasya svata evānubhavamātrātmakatvāt. ata eva sarvapramāṇāvatārāsaṃbhavaṃ vakṣyati. pramāṇavyavasthāyāś cānubhavamātrāśrayatvāt. ata āha

vākyaikagamyaṃ yad vastu nānyasmāt tatra viśvaset
nā'prameye svatassiddhe'visvāsaḥ katham ātmani (89)

yad apy uktaṃ, "antareṇa vidhim" iti, tad apy abuddhipūrvakam iva naḥ pratibhāti. yasmāt kālāntaraphaladāyiṣu karmasv etad ghaṭate. ātmalābhakāla eva phaladāyini tv ātmajñāne naitat samañjasam ity āha

jñānāt phale hy avāpte'smin pratyakṣe bhavaghātini
upakārāya tan neti na nyāyyaṃ bhāti no vacaḥ (90)

yadapi jaiminīyaṃ vacanamudghāṭayasi, tadapi tadvivakṣā'parijñānād evodbhāvyate. kiṃ kāraṇam? yato na jaiminer ayam abhiprāya āmnāyaḥ sarva eva kriyārtha iti. yadi hy ayam abhiprāyo'bhaviṣyat, "athāto brahmajijñāsā. jadmādy asya yataḥ". ity evam ādi brahmavastusvarūpamātrayāthātmyaprakāśanaparaṃ gambhīranyāyasaṃdṛbdhaṃ sarvavedāntārthamīmāṃsanaṃ śrimaccharīrakaṃ nāsūtrayiṣyat. asūtrayac ca. tasmāj jaiminer evāyam abhiprāyo yathaiva vidhivākyānāṃ svārthamātre prāmāṇyam, evam aikātmyavākyānām apy, anadhigatavastuparicchedasāmyād iti. ata idam abhidhīyate.

adhicodanaṃ ya āmnayās tasyaiva syāt kriyārthatā
tattvamasyādivākyānāṃbrūta karmārthatā katham (91)

api ca, aikātmyapakṣa ivādṛṣṭārthakarmasu bhavatpakṣe'pi pravṛttirdurlakṣyā. yataḥ

svargam yiyāsur juhuyād agnihotraṃ yathāvidhi
dehād vyutthāpitasyaivaṃ kartṛtvam jaimineḥ katham (92)

na ca pratyākhyātāśeṣaśarīrādikarmasādhanasvabhāvasyātmamātrasya karmasv adhikāraḥ yasmāt.

sarvapramāṇāsaṃbhāvyo hy ahaṃvṛttyaikasādhanaḥ
yuṣmad artham anāditsur jaiminiḥ preryate katham (93)

pravṛttikāraṇābhāvāc ca. yasmāt

sukhaduḥkhādibhir yoga ātmano nāhamekṣyate
parāktvāt pratyagātmatvāj jaiminiḥ preryate katham (94)

kiṃca

na tāvad yoga evāsti śarīreṇātmanaḥ sadā
viṣayair dūrato nāsti svargādau syāt kathaṃ sukham (95)

yasmād anyathā nopapadyate

narābhimāninaṃ tasmāt kārakādyātmadarśinam
mantra āhorarīkṛtya "kurvam" iti na nirdvayam (96)

yac coktaṃ "virahayya" iti tadapi na samyag eva. tathāpi tu na yā kācit kriyā yatra kva cādhyāharaṇīyā, kiṃ tu yā yatrābhipretasaṃbandhaṃ ghaṭayituṃ śaknoty ākāṅkṣāṃ ca vākyasya pūrayati saivādhyāharaṇīyā. evaṃviśiṣṭā ca kriyāsmābhir abhyupagataiva. sā tūpāditsitavākyārthāvirodhiny eva, nābhātārthaprādurbhāvaphaleti. ṣaḍbhāvavikārarahitātmavastuno nirdhātāśeṣadvaitānarthasyāparādhīnaprakāśasya vijijñāpayiṣitatvād "asy" "asmi" ityādikriyāpadaṃsvamahimsiddhārthapratipādanasamarthamabhyupagantavyaṃ, na viparītārthapratipādanaparam iti

dhāved iti na dānārthe padaṃ yadvat prayujyate
edhītyādi tathā necchet svataḥ siddhārthavācini (97)

na ca yathoktavastuvṛttapratipādanavyatirekeṇa tattvamasyādivākyaṃ vākyārthāntaraṃ vaktīti śakyam adhyavasātum ity āha

tattvamasyādivākyānāṃ svatassiddhārthabodhanāt
arthāntaraṃ na saṃdraṣṭuṃ śakyate tridaśair api (98)

yasmād evam

ataḥ sarvāśramāṇāṃ tu vāṇmanaḥkāyakarmabhiḥ
svanuṣṭhitair na muktiḥ syāj jñānād eva hi sā yataḥ (99)

tasmāc ca kāraṇādetad apy upapannam

svamanorathasaṃkḷptaprajñādhmātadhiyām ataḥ
śrotriyeṣv eva vācas tāḥ śobhante nātmavediṣu (100)

CHAPTER TWO

dvitīyo'dhyāyaḥ

pratyakṣādinām anevaṃviṣayatvāt, teṣāṃ svārambhakaviṣayopanipātitvād, ātmanaś cāśeṣaprameyavailakṣaṇyāt, sarvānarthaikahetvajñānāpanodijñānadivākarodayahetutvaṃ vastumātrayāthātmyaprakāśanapaṭīyasas tattvamasyāder vacasa eveti bahvībhir upapattibhiḥ pradarśitam. atas tadarthāpratipattau yat kāraṇaṃ tadapanayanāya dvitīyo' dhyāya ārabhyate

śrāvito vetti vākyārthaṃ na cet tattvamasīty ataḥ
tvaṃpadārthānabhijñatvād atas tatprakriyocyate (1)

yo'yam ahaṃ brahmeti vākyārthas tatpratipattir vākyād eveti pratyakṣādinām anevaṃviṣayatvād ity avādiṣaṃ tasya viśuddhyartham anaikāntikatvaṃpūrvapakṣatvenopasthāpyate

kṛtsnānātmanivṛttau ca kaścid āpnoti nirvṛtim
śrutavākyasmṛteś cānyaḥ smāryate ca vaco'paraḥ (2)

etatprasaṅgena śrotrantaropanyāsam ubhayatrāpi saṃbhāvanāyāha

vākyaśravaṇamātrāc ca piśācakavad āpnuyāt
triṣu yādṛcchikī siddhiḥ smāryamāṇe tu niścitā (3)

nāyam anaikāntiko hetuḥ. yataḥ

sarvo'yaṃ mahimā jñeyo vākyasyaiva yathoditaḥ
vākyārthaṃ na hy ṛte vākyāt kaścij jānāti tattvataḥ (4)

vākyaṃ ca pratipādanāya pravṛttaṃ sat pratipādayaty eva, sarvapramāṇānām apy evaṃvṛttatvāt ·

nāhaṃgrāhye na taddhīne na pratyaṅ nāpi duḥkhini
virodhaḥ sad asīty asmād vākyābhijñasya jāyate (5)

nāviraktasya saṃsārān nivivṛtsā tato bhavet
na cānivṛttatṛṣṇasya puruṣasya mumukṣutā (6)

na cāmumukṣor astīha gurupādopasarpaṇam
na vinā gurusaṃbandhaṃ vākyasya śravaṇaṃ bhavet (7)

tathā padapadārthau ca na sto vākyam ṛte kvacit
anvayavyatirekau ca tāv ṛte stāṃ kimāśrayau (8)

anvayavyatirekābhyāṃ vinā vākyārthabodhanam
na syāt tena vināj̃ñānaprahāṇaṃ nopapadyate (9)

vināj̃ñānaprahāṇena puruṣārthaḥ sudurlabhaḥ
tasmād yathoktasiddhyarthaṃ paro grantho'vatāryate (10)

varcaskaṃ tv annakāryatvād yathā nātmeti gamyate
tadbhāgaḥ sendriyo dehastadvat kimiti nekṣyate (11)

ādyantayor anātmatve prasiddhe madhye'pi kaḥ pratibandhaḥ?

prāg anātmaiva jagdhaṃ sad ātmatām ety avidyayā
sragālepanavad dehaṃ tasmāt paśyed viviktadhīḥ (12)

athaivam api madvacanaṃ nādriyase, svayam evaitasmāccharīrād aśucirāśer nirāśo bhaviṣyasi

manyase tāvad asmīti yāvad asmān na nīyase
śvabhiḥ kroḍīkṛte dehe naivaṃ tvam abhimaṃsyase (13)

śira ākramya pādena bhartsayaty aparān śunaḥ
dṛṣṭvā sādhāraṇaṃ dehaṃ kasmāt sakto'si tatra bhoḥ (14)

śrutiparīprāpito'yam artho'nātmā buddhyādidehānta itīdam āha

busavrīhipalālāṃśair bījam ekaṃ tridhā yathā
buddhimāṃsapurīṣāṃśair annaṃ tadvad avasthitam (15)

yathoktārthapratipattau satyāṃ, na rāgadveṣābhyāṃ vikriyate vipaścid ity asyārthasya pratipattaye dṛṣṭāntaḥ

varcaske saṃparityakte doṣataś cāvadhārite
yadi doṣaṃ vadet tasmai kiṃ tatroccariturbhavet (16)

tadvat sūkṣme tathā sthūle dehe tyakte vivekataḥ
yadi doṣaṃ vadet tābhyāṃ kiṃ tatra viduṣo bhavet (17)

etāvad eva hy "ahaṃ brahmāsmi" iti vākyārthāpratipattau kāraṇaṃ yaduta buddhyādau dehānte hy ahaṃ mameti nissandhibandhano grahaḥ. tadvyatireke hi na kutaścid-vibhajyata, ekala eva pratyagātmany avatiṣṭhata ity āha
ripau bandhau svadehe ca samaikātmyaṃ prapaśyataḥ
vivekinaḥ kutaḥ kopaḥ svadehāvayaveṣv iva (18)

itaś cānātmā dehādiḥ

ghaṭādivac ca dṛśyatvat tair eva karaṇair dṛśeḥ
svapne cānanvayāj jñeyo deho'nātmeti sūribhiḥ (19)

dehādikāryakaraṇasaṃghātavyatirekāvyatirekadarśinaḥ pratyakṣata eva viruddhaṃ kāryam upalabhyate

caturbhir uhyate yat tat sarvaśaktyā śarīrakam
tūlāyate tad evāhaṃdhiyāghrātam ascetasām (20)

prasiddhatvāt prakaraṇārthopasaṃhārāyāha

sthūlaṃ yuktyā nirasyaivaṃ nabhaso nilatām iva
dehaṃ sūkṣmaṃ nirākuryād ato yuktibhir ātmanaḥ (21)

kathaṃ dehaṃ sūkṣmaṃ nirākuryād iti? ucyate

ahaṃmamatva yatnecchā nātmadharmāḥ kṛśatvavat
karmatvenopalabhyatvād apāyitvac ca vastravat (22)

vaidharmye dṛṣṭāntaḥ

noṣṇimānaṃ dahaty agniḥ svarūpatvād yathā jvalan
tathaivātmātmano vidyād ahaṃ naivāviśeṣataḥ (23)

ekasyātmanaḥ karmakartṛbhāvaḥ sarvathā nopapadyata iti śrutvā, mīmāṃsakaḥ pratyavatiṣṭhate, ahaṃpratyayagrāhyatvād grāhyagrāhaka ātmeti. tannivṛttyartham āha

yatkarmako hi yo bhāvo nāsau tatkartṛko yataḥ
ghaṭapratyayavat tasmān nāhaṃ syād draṣṭṛkarmakaḥ (24)

atrāha pratyakṣeṇātmanaḥ karmakartṛtvābhyupagame tatpādopajīvinānumānena pratyakṣotsāraṇam ayuktam iti codyaṃ. tannirākaraṇāya pratyakṣopanyāsaḥ

yatra yo dṛśyate draṣṭrā tasyaivāsau guṇo na tu
draṣṭṛstham dṛśyatāṃ yasmān naiveyād draṣṭṛbodhavat (25)

pratyakṣenaiva bhavadabhimatasya pratyakṣasyābhāsi-kṛtatvāt sustham evānumānam. atas tad eva prakriyate. tatra ca vikalpadūṣaṇābhidhānam

nātmanā na tadaṃśena guṇaḥ svastho'vagamyate
abhinnatvāt samatvāc ca niraṃśatvād akarmataḥ (26)

na yugapan nāpi krameṇobhayathā caikasya dharmiṇo grāhyagrāhakatvam upapadyata iti pratipādanāyāha

draṣṭṛtvenopayuktatvāt tadaiva syān na dṛśyatā
kālāntare ced dṛśyatvaṃ na hy adraṣṭṛkam iṣyate (27)

santu kāmam anātmadharmā mamatvādayo yathoktanyāya-balād anātmatayaiva ca teṣu vyavahārād ahaṃrūpasya tu pratyagātmasaṃbandhitayaiva prasiddher, "aham brahmāsmi" iti śruteś cānātmadharmatvamayuktamiti cet, tan na

ahaṃdharmas tv abhinnaś ced ahaṃ brahmeti vākyataḥ
gauro'ham ity anaikānto vākyaṃ tadvyapanetṛ tat (28)

kathaṃ vākyaṃ tadvyapanetṛ tad iti? ucyate

yo'yaṃ sthāṇuḥ pumān eṣa puṃdhiyā sthāṇudhīr iva
brahmāsmīti dhiyā'śeṣā hy ahaṃbuddhir nivartyate (29)

ahaṃparicchedavyāvṛttau na kiṃcid avyāvṛttam dvaita-jātam avaśiṣyate, dvitīyasaṃbandhasya tanmūlatvāt. ata āha

nivṛttāyām ahaṃbuddhau mamadhīḥ pravilīyate
ahaṃbījā hi sā sidhyet tamo'bhāve kutaḥ phaṇī (30)

vivakṣitadṛṣṭāntāṃśajñāpanāya dṛṣṭāntavyākhyā

tamo'bhibūtacitto hi rajjvāṃ paśyati roṣaṇam
bhrāntyā, bhrāntyā vinā tasmān noragaṃ sraji vīkṣate (31)

ananvayāc ca nātmadharmo'haṃkāraḥ

ātmanaś ced ahaṃdharmo yāyān muktisuṣuptayoḥ
yato nānveti tenāyam anyadīyo bhaved aham (32)

ātmadharmatvābhyupagame'parihāryadoṣaprasaktiś ca

yady ātmadharmo'haṃkāro nityatvaṃ tasya bodhavat
nityatve mokṣaśāstrāṇāṃ vaiyarthyaṃ prāpnuyād
dhruvam (33)

syāt parihāraḥ svābhavikadharmatvābhyupagame'py āmrādiphalavad iti cet, tan na

āmrādeḥ pariṇāmitvād guṇahānir guṇāntaraiḥ
avikāri tu tad brahma na hi draṣṭur iti śruteḥ (34)

ahaṃkārasya cāgamāpāyitvāt, taddharmiṇaś cānityatvaṃ prāpnoti

āgamāpāyiniṣṭhatvād anityatvam iyād dṛśiḥ
upayann apayan dharmo vikaroti hi dharmiṇam (35)

astv anityatvaṃ kam upālabhemahi pramāṇopapannatvād iti cet, tan na

sadā'viluptasākṣitvaṃ svatassiddhaṃ na pāryate
apahnotuṃ ghaṭasyeva kuśāgrīyadhiyātmanaḥ (36)

etasmāc ca hetor ahaṃkārasyānātmadharmatvam-avasīyatām

pramāṇaiścāvagamyatvād ghaṭādivad ahaṃdṛśeḥ
yato rāddhiḥ pramāṇānāṃ sa kathaṃ taih prasidhyati (37)

dharmadharmiṇoś cetaretaraviruddhātmakatvād asaṅgatiḥ

dharmiṇaśca viruddhatvān na dṛśyaguṇasaṅgatiḥ
mārutāndolitajvālaṃ śaityaṃ nāgniṃ sisṛpsati (38)

tasmād visrabdham upagamyatām

draṣṭṛtvaṃ dṛśyatā caiva naikasminn ekadā kvacit
dṛśyadṛśyo na ca draṣṭā draṣṭur darśī dṛśir na ca (39)

sarvasaṃvyavahāralopaśca prāpnoti. yasmāt

draṣṭāpi yadi dṛśyāyā ātmeyāt karmatāṃ dhiyaḥ
yaugapadyam adṛśyatvaṃ vaiyarthyaṃ cāpnuyāc chrutiḥ (40)

kutaḥ? yasmāt

nāluptadṛṣṭer dṛśyatvaṃ dṛśyatve draṣṭṛtā kutaḥ
syāc ced dṛg ekaṃ nirdṛśyaṃ jagad vā syād asākṣikam (41)

uktayuktiṃ dṛḍhīkartum āgamodāharaṇopanyāsaḥ

ārtam anyad dṛśeḥ sarvaṃ "neti netīti" cāsakṛt
vadantī nirguṇaṃ brahma kathaṃ śrutir upekṣyate (42)

"mahābhūtāny ahaṃkāra" ity etat kṣetram ucyate
na dṛśer dvaitayogo'sti viśveśvaramatād api (43)

adhunā prakṛtārthopasaṃhāraḥ

evam etadd hirug jñeyaṃ mithyāsiddham anātmakam
mohamūlaṃ sudurbodhaṃ dvaitaṃ yuktibhir ātmanaḥ (44)

kuto mithyāsiddhatvaṃ dvaitasyeti cet

na pṛthaṅ nātmanā siddhir ātmano'nyasya vastunaḥ
ātmavat kalpitas tasmād ahaṃkārādir ātmani (45)

tasmād ajñānavijṛmbhitam etat

dṛśyāḥ śabdādayaḥ kḷptā draṣṭṛ ca brahma nirguṇam
ahaṃ tad ubhayaṃ bibhrad bhrāntim ātmani yacchati (46)

tata eveyam abhinnasyātmano bhedabuddhiḥ

dṛg eka sarvabhūteṣu bhāti dṛśyair anekavat
jalabhājanabhedena mayūkhasragvibhedavat (47)

yathoktārthasya pratipattaye dṛṣṭāntaḥ

mitrodāsīnaśatrutvaṃ yathaikasyānyakalpanāt
abhinnasya cites tadvad bhedo'ntaḥkaraṇāśrayaḥ (48)

apahāro yathā bhānoḥ sarvato jalapātrakaiḥ
tatkriyākṛtideśāptis tathā buddhibhir ātmanaḥ (49)

na ca viruddhadharmāṇām ekatrānupapattiḥ. kiṃ kāraṇam?

kalpitānām avastutvāt syād ekatrāpi saṃbhavaḥ
kamanīyā'śuciḥ svādvīty ekasyām iva yoṣiti (50)

na cāyaṃ kriyākārakaphalātmaka ābhāsa īṣad api paramārthavastu spṛśati, tasya mohamātropādānatvāt

abhūtābhiniveśena svātmānaṃ vañcayaty ayam
asaty api dvitīye'rthe somaśarmapitā yathā (51)

vastuyāthātmyānavabodhapaṭalāvanaddhākṣaḥ san

subhrūḥ sunāsā sumukhī sunetrā cāruhāsinī
kalpanāmātrasaṃmohād rāmety āliṅgate'śucim (52)

sarvasyānarthajātasya jihāsitasya mūlam ahaṃkāra eva, tasyātmānātmoparāgāt. na tu paramārthata ātmano 'vidyayā tatkāryeṇa vā saṃbandho'bhūd, asti, bhaviṣyati vā, tasyāpariluptadṛṣṭisvābhāvyāt

dṛśyānuraktaṃ taddraṣṭṛ dṛśyam draṣṭranurañjitam
ahaṃvṛttyobhayaṃ raktaṃ tannāśe'dvaitātmanaḥ (53)

iha kecic codayanti yo'yam anvayavyatirekābhyām anātmatyotsārito'haṃkāro vākyārthapratipattaye, so'yaṃ viparītārthaḥ saṃvṛtto, yasmād "ahaṃ brahmāsmi" iti brahmāhampadārthayoḥ sāmānādhikaraṇyaśravaṇād anātmārthena sāmānādhikaraṇyaṃ prāpnoti. vaktavyā ca pratyagātmani tasya vṛttir iti. socyate prasiddhalakṣaṇāguṇavṛttibhiḥ

nājñāsiṣam iti prāha suṣuptād utthito'pi hi
ayodāh ādi vat tena lakṣaṇaṃ paramātmanaḥ (54)

pratyaktvād atiūkṣmatvād ātmadṛṣṭyanuśīlanāt
ato vṛttīr vihāyānyā hy ahaṃvṛttyopalakṣyate (55)

ātmanā cāvinābhāvam atha vā vilayaṃ vrajet
na tu pakṣāntaraṃ yāyād ataś cāh aṃdhiyocyate (56)

kīdṛk punar vastu lakṣyam

nāmādibhyaḥ paro bhūmā niṣkalo'kārako'kriyaḥ
sa evātmavatām ātmā svatas siddhaḥ sa eva naḥ (57)

ajñānotthabuddhyādikartṛtvopādhim ātmānaṃ parigṛhyaivānvayavyatirekābhyām "ahaṃ sukhī duḥkhī ca" ityahaṃkārāder anātmadharmatvamuktaṃ. kevalātmābhyupagame'śakyatvāt phalābhāvāc ca. athedānīm avidyāparikalpitaṃ sākṣitvam āśritya kartṛtvādyaśeṣapariṇāmapratiṣedhāyātha

eṣa sarvadhiyāṃ vṛttam aviluptaikadarśanaḥ
vīkṣate'vikṣamāṇo'pi nimiṣat tad dhruvo'dhruvam (58)

nanu sarvasiddhāntānām api svasvadṛṣṭyapekṣayopapannatvād, itaretaradṛṣṭyapekṣayā dussthitasiddhikatvān, naikatrāpi viśvāsaṃ paśyāmo. na ca sarvatārkikair adūṣitaṃ samarthitaṃ, sarvatārkikopadravāpasarpaṇāya vartma saṃbhāvayāmaḥ. ucyate. visrabdhaiḥ saṃbhāvyatām anubhavamātraśaraṇatvāt sarvaptārkikaprasthānānām. tadabhidhīyate

imaṃ prāśnikam uddiśya tarkajvarabhṛśāturāḥ
tvācchiraskavacojālair mohayantītaretaram (59)

atrāpi codayanti. anubhavātmano'pi vikriyābhyupagame'nabhyupagame'pi doṣa eva. yasmād āha

"varṣātapābhyāṃ kiṃ vyomnaś carmaṇy eva tayoḥ phalaṃ
carmopamaś cet so'nityaḥ khytulyaś ced asatsamaḥ" (60)

buddhijanmani puṃsaś ca vikṛtir yady anityatā
athāvikṛtir evāyaṃ pramāteti na yujyate (61)

asya parihāraḥ

ūrdhvaṃ gacchati dhūme khaṃ bhidyate svin na bhidyate
na bhidyate cet sthāsnutvaṃ bhidyate ced bhidā'sya kā (62)

ity etatpratipattyartham āha

avikriyasya bhoktṛtvaṃ syād ahaṃbuddhivibhramāt
na t yānavibhramād yadvan nageṣu gatikalpanam (63)

yathoktārthāviṣkaraṇāya dṛṣṭāntantaropādānam

yathā jātyamaṇeḥ śubhrā jvalantī niścalā śikhā
saṃnidhyasaṃnidhāneṣu ghaṭādhīnām avikriyā (64)

ayam atrāṃśo vivakṣita iti jñāpanāyāha

yadavasthā vyanaktīti tadavasthaiva sā punaḥ
bhaṇyate na vyanaktīti ghaṭādīnām asaṃnidhau (65)

tatra ca

sarvadhīvyañjakas tadvat paramātmā pradīpakaḥ
saṃnidhyasaṃnidhāneṣu dhīvṛttīnām avikriyaḥ (66)

na prakāśakriyā kācid asya svātmani vidyate
upacārāt kriyā sā 'sya yaḥ prakāśyasya saṃnidhiḥ (67)

maivaṃ śaṅkiṣṭhāḥ sāṃkhyarāddhānto'yam iti. yataḥ

yathā viśuddha ākāśe sahasaivābhramaṇḍalam
bhūtvā vilīyate tadvad ātmanihākhilaṃ jagat (68)

tasmād eṣa kūṭastho na dvaitaṃ manāg api spṛśati. yataḥ

śabdādyākāranirbhāsāḥ kṣaṇapradhvaṃsinīr dṛśā
nityo'kramadṛg ātmaiko vyāpnotīva dhiyo'niśam (69)

evaṃ ca sati buddheḥ pariṇāmitvaṃ yuktam

atītānāgatehatyān yugapat sarvagocarān
vetty ātmavan na dhir yasmāt teneyaṃ pariṇāaminī (70)

tataś caitat siddham

apaśyan paśyatīṃ buddhim aśṛṇvan śṛṇvatīṃ tathā
niryatno'vikriyo'nicchann icchantīṃ cāpy aluptadṛk (71)

dviṣantīm adviṣann ātmā kupyantīṃ capy akopanaḥ
nirduḥkho duḥkhinīṃ caiva nissukhaḥ sukhinīm api (72)

amuhyamāno muhyantīṃ kalpayantīm akalpayan
smarantīm asmaraṃś caiva śayānām asvapan muhuḥ (73)

sarvākārāṃ nirākāraḥ svārtho'svārthāṃ niriṅganaḥ
nistrikālas trikālasthāṃkūṭasthaḥ kṣaṇabhaṅgurām (74)

nirapekṣaś ca sāpekṣāṃ parācīṃ pratyag advayaḥ.
sāvadhiṃ nirgateyattaḥ sarvadeheṣu paśyati (75)

etasmāc ca kāraṇād ayam artho vyavasīyatām

duḥkhī yadi bhaved ātmā kas sākṣī duḥkhino bhavet
duḥkhinaḥ sākṣitā'yuktā sākṣiṇoduḥkhitā tathā (76)

pūrvasyaiva vyākhyānārtham āha

narte syād vikriyāṃduḥkhī sākṣitā kā vikāriṇaḥ
dhīvikriyāsahasrāṇāṃ sākṣy ato'ham avikriyaḥ(77)

evaṃ sarvasmin vyabhicāriṇy ātmavastvevāvyabhicāity anubhavato vyavasthāpanāyāha

pramāṇatannibheṣv asyā nocchittir mama saṃvidaḥ
matto'nyad rūpam ābhāti yat tat syāt kṣaṇapbhaṅgi hi (78)

utpattisthitibhaṅgeṣu kumbhasya viyato yathā
notpattisthitināśās syur buddher evaṃ mamāpi ca (79)

sukhaduḥkhatatsaṃbandhānāṃ ca pratyakṣatvān na śraddhāmātragrāhyam etat

sukhaduḥkhādisaṃbaddhāṃ yathā daṇḍena daṇḍinam
rādhako vikṣate buddhiṃ sākṣī tadvad asaṃhataḥ (80)

etasmāc ca hetor dhiyaḥ pariṇāmitvaṃ yuktam

yenaivāsyā bhaved yogaḥ sukhakumbhādinā dhiyaḥ
taṃ vidanti tadaivānyaṃ vetti nāto vikāriṇī (81)

asyāś ca kṣaṇabhaṅguratve svayam evātmā sākṣi. na hi kūṭasthāvabodham antareṇa buddher evāvirbhāvatirobhāvādisiddhir asti

pariṇāmidhiyāṃ vṛttaṃ nityākramadṛgātmanā
ṣaḍbhāvavikriyām eti vyāptaṃ khenāṅkuro yathā (82)

sata ātmanaś cāvikāritve yuktiḥ

smṛtisvapnaprabodheṣu na kaścit pratyayo dhiyaḥ
dṛśāvyāpto'sty ato nityam avikārī svayaṃ dṛśh (83)

evaṃ tāvat parābhyupagataprakriyāprasthānena nirastāśeṣavikāraikātmyaṃ pratipāditam upapattibhiḥ. athādhnā śrautīṃ prakriyām avalambyocyate

astu vā pariṇāmo'sya dṛśeḥ kūṭastharūpataḥ
kalpito'pi mṛṣaivāsau daṇḍasyevāpsu vakratā (84)

ṣaṭsu bhāvavikāreṣu niṣiddheṣv evam ātmani
doṣaḥ kaścid ihāsaktuṃ na śakyas tārkikaśvabhiḥ (85)

prakṛtam evopādāya buddheḥ pariṇāmitvam ātmanaś ca kūṭasthatvaṃ yuktibhir ucyate

praty arthaṃ tu vibhidyante buddhayo viṣayonmukhāḥ
na bhidā'vagates tadvat sarvās tāś cinnibhā yataḥ (86)

svasaṃbaddhārtha eva
sāvaśeṣaparicchediny ata eva na kṛtsnavit

sāvaśeṣaparicchediny ata eva na kṛtsnavit
no cet pariṇamed buddhiḥ sarvajñā svātmavad bhavet (87)

ato'vagater ekatvāt

caṇḍālabuddher yad draṣṭṛ tad eva brahmabuddhidṛk
ekaṃ tad ubhayor jyotir bhāsyabhedād anekavat (88)

kasmāt?

avasthādeśakālādibhedo nāsty anayor yataḥ
tasmāj jagaddhiyāṃ vṛttaṃ jyotir ekaṃ sadekṣate (89)

sarvadeheṣv ātmaikatve pratibuddhaparamārthatattvasyāpy apratibuddhadehasaṃbandhād aśeṣaduḥkhasaṃbandha iti cet, tan na

bodhāt prāg api duḥkhitvaṃ nānyadehottham asti naḥ
bodhād ūrdhvaṃ kutas tat syād yatra svagatam apy asat (90)

na ceyaṃ svamanīṣiketi grāhyam. kutaḥ? śrutyavaṣṭambhāt

śabdādyākāranirbhāsā hānopādānadharmiṇī
bhāsyety āha śrutir dṛṣṭir ātmano'pariṇāminaḥ (91)

kā tv asau śrutiḥ?

"dṛṣṭer draṣṭāram" ātmānaṃ na paśyer dṛśyamānayā
"vijñātāram are kena vijānīyād" dhiyāṃ patim (92)

yasmāt sarvapramāṇopapanno'yam arthas tasmād ato'nyathāvādino jātyandhā ivānukampanīyā ity āha

tad etad advayaṃ brahma nirvikāraṃ kubuddhibhiḥ
jātyandhagajadṛṣṭyeva koṭiśaḥ parikalpyate (93)

pramāṇopapannasyārthasya asaṃbhāvanāt tadanukampanīyatvasiddhiḥ. tad etad āha

yady viśeṣaṇaṃ dṛṣṭaṃ nātmanas tad ananvayāt
khasya kumbhādivat tasmād ātmā syān nirviśeṣaṇaḥ (94)

ataś cātmano bhedāsaṃsparśo bhedasya mithyāsvābhāvyād ata āha

avagatyātmano yasmād āgamāpāyi kumbhavat
sāhaṃkāram idaṃ viśvaṃ tasmāt tat syāt kacādivat (95)

sarvasyaivānumāṇavyāpārasya phalam iyad eva yadvivekagrahaṇaṃ. tad ucyate

buddher anātmadharmatvam anumānāt prasiddhyati
ātmano'py advitīyatvam ātmatvād eva siddhyati (96)

yadyapy ayaṃ grahītṛgrahaṇagrāhyagṛhītitatphalātmaka ābrahmastambaparyantaḥ saṃsāro'nvayavyatirekābhyām anātmatayā nirmālyavadapaviddhaḥ. tathāpi tu naivāsau svatassiddhātmavyatiriktānātmaprakṛtipadārthavyapāśrayaḥ sāṃkhyānām iva. kiṃ tarhi? svatassiddhānuditānastamitakūṭasthātmaprajñānamātraśarīrapratibimbitāvicāritasiddhātmānavabodhāśraya eva, tadupādānatvāt tasya, itimam artham nirvaktukāma āha

ṛte jñānaṃ na santy arthā asti jñānam ṛte'pi tān
evaṃ dhiyo hirugjyotir vivicyād anumānataḥ (97)

yasmāt pramāṇaprameyavyavahāra ātmānavabodhāśraya eva, tasmāt siddham ātmano'prameyatvam. naiva hi kāryaṃ svakāraṇam atilaṅghyānyatrākāraka āspadam upanibadhnāti. ata āha

vyavadhīyanta evāmi buddhidehaghaṭādayaḥ
ātmatvād ātmanaḥ kena vyavadhānaṃ manāg api (98)

svayam anavagamātmakatvād, anavagamātmakatvaṃ ca mohamātropādānatvāt

pramāṇam antareṇaiṣāṃ buddhyādīnām asiddhatā
anubhūtiphalārthitvād ātmājñaḥ kim apekṣate (99)

vakṣyamāṇetaretarādhyāsasiddhyarthamuktavyatirekānuvādaḥ

ghaṭabuddher ghaṭāc cārthād draṣṭur yadvadvibhinnatā
ahaṃbuddher ahaṃgamyād duḥkhinaś ca tathā dṛśeḥ (100)

evam etayor ātmānātmanoḥ svataḥ parataḥ siddhayor, laukikarajjusarpādhyāropavad avidyopāśraya evataretarādhyāropa ity etad āha

abhrayānaṃ yātha mohāc chaśabhṛty adhyavasyati
sukhitvādin dhiyo dharmāṃs tadvadātmani manyate (101)

dagdhṛtvaṃ ca yathā vahner ayaso manyate kudhīḥ
caitanyaṃ tadvad ātmīyaṃ mohāt kartari manyate (102)

sarva evāyam ātmānātmavibhāgaḥ pratyakṣādipramāṇavartmany anupatito'vidyotsaṅgavarty eva na paramātmavyapāśrayaḥ. asyāś cāvidyāyāḥ sarvānarthahetoḥ kuto nivṛttir iti cet, tad āha

duḥkharāśer vicitrasya seyaṃ bhrāntiś cirantanī
mūlaṃ saṃsāravṛkṣasya tadbādhastattvadarśanāt (103)

tadbādhas tattvadarśanād iti kutaḥ saṃbhāvyata iti ced, ata āha āgopālāvipālapaṇḍitam iyam eva prasiddhiḥ

apramotthaṃ pramotthena jñānaṃ jñānena bādhyate
ahirajjvādivadbādho dehādy ātmamates tathā (104)

laukikaprameyavailakṣaṇyād ātmano nehānadhigatādhigamaḥ pramāṇaphalam

avidyānāśamātraṃ tu phalam ity upacaryate
nājñātajñāpanaṃ nyāyyam avagatyekarūpataḥ (105)

yasmād ātmānavabodhamātropādānāḥ pramātrādayas, tasmāt

na vidanty ātmanaḥ sattāṃ draṣṭṛdarśanagocarāḥ
na cānyonyamato'miṣāṃ jñeyatvaṃ bhinnasādhanam (106)

draṣṭrāder asādhāraṇarūpajñāpanāyāha

bāhya ākāravān grāhyo grahaṇaṃ niścayādimat
anvayy aham iti jñeyaḥ sākṣi tv ātmā dhruvaḥ sadā (107)

sarvakārakakriyāphalavibhāgātmakasaṃsāraśūnya ātmeti, kārakakriyāphalavibhāgasākṣitvād ātmanas, tad āha

grāhakagrahaṇagrāhyavibhāge yo'vibhāgavān
hānopādānayos sākṣi hānopādānavarjitaḥ (108)

grāhakādiniṣṭhaiva grāhakādibhāvābhāvavibhāgasiddhiḥ kasmān neti cet, tad āha

svasādhanaṃ svayaṃ naṣṭo na nāśaṃ vetty abhāvataḥ
ata eva na cānyeṣām ato'sau bhinnasākṣikaḥ (109)

grāhakāder anyasākṣipūrvakatvasiddheḥ svasākṣiṇo'py-anyasākṣipūrvakatvād anavastheti cet, tan na sākṣiṇo vyatiriktahetvanapekṣatvād ata āha

dhīvannāpekṣate siddhim ātmāny asmād avikriyaḥ
nirapekṣam apekṣyaiva siddhyanty anye na tu svayam (110)

yato grāhakādiṣv ātmabhāvo'vidyānibandhana eva, tasmād anvayavyatirekābhyāṃ vibhajyānātmanaḥ, svayam

utpattisthitināśeṣu yo'vagatyaiva vartate
jagato'vikārayā'vehi tam asmīti na naśvaram (111)

svatassiddhātmacaitanyapratibimbitāvicāritasiddhikātmā-navabodhotthetaretarasvabhāvapekṣasiddhatvāt svataś cāsiddher anātmano dvaitendrajālasya

na svayam svasya nānātvaṃ nāvagatyātmanā yataḥ
nobhābhyām apy atas siddham advaitaṃ dvaitabādhayā (112)

yathoktārthapratipattidraḍhimne śrutyudāharaṇopanyāsaḥ

nityāvagatirūpatvāt kārakādir na cātmanaḥ
"asthūlaṃ" "neti neti"iti "na jāyata" iti śrutiḥ (113)

sarvasyāsya grāhakāder dvaitaprapañcasyātmānavabodhamātropādānasya svayaṃ seddhum aśakyatvād, ātmasiddheś cānupādeyatvāt

ātmanaś cen nivāryante buddhidehaghaṭādayaḥ
ṣaṣṭhagocarakalpās te vijñeyāḥ paramārthataḥ (114)

kuto nyāyabalād evaṃ niścitaṃ pratīyate? yasmāt

nityāṃ saṃvidam āśritya svatas siddhām avikriyām
siddhāyante dhiyo bodhās tāṃś cāśritya ghaṭādayaḥ (115)

yasmān na kayācid api yuktya ātmanaḥ kārakatvaṃ kriyātvaṃ phalatvaṃ copapadyate, tasmād ātmavastuyathātmyānavabodhamātropādānatvān nabhasīva rajodhūmatuṣāranīhāranīlatvādyadhyāso, yathoktātmani sarvo'yaṃ kriyākārakaphalātmakasaṃsāro'haṃmamatvayatnecchādimithyādhyāsa eveti siddham imam artham āha

ahaṃmithyābhiśāpena duḥkhy ātmā tadbubhutsayā
itaḥ śrutiṃ tayā netiyuktaḥ kaivalyam āsthitaḥ (116)

tasyāsya mumukṣoḥ śrautād vacasaḥ svapnanimittotsāritanidrasyeveyaṃ niścitārthā pramā jāyate

nāhaṃ na ca mamātmatvāt sarvadānātmavarjitaḥ
bhānāv iva tamodhyāso'pahnavaś ca tathā mayi (117)

so'yam evaṃpratipannasvabhāvam ātmānaṃ pratipanno'nukrośati

yatra tv asyeti sāṭopaṃ kṛtsnadvaitaniṣedhinīm
protsārayantīṃ saṃsāram apya śrauṣaṃ na kiṃ śrutim (118)

ity om ity avabuddhātmā niṣkalo'kārako'kriyaḥ
virakta iva buddhyāder ekākitvam upeyivān (119)

CHAPTER THREE

tṛtīyo'dhyāyaḥ

sarvo'yaṃ pramitipramāṇaprameyapramātṛlakṣaṇa, ābrahmastambaparyanto mithyādhyāsa eveti bahuśa upapattibhir atiṣṭhipam. ātmā ca janmādiṣaḍbhāvavikāravarjitaḥ kūṭasthabodha eveti sphuṭīkṛtam. tayoś ca mithyādhyāsa-kūṭasthātmanor nāntareṇājñānaṃ saṃbandho'nyatra codanā-pariprāpitāt yathā "iyam evarg agniḥ sāma" iti. tac cājñānaṃ svātmamātranimittaṃ na saṃbhavatīti kasyacit kasmiṃścid- viṣaye bhavatīty abhyupagantavyam. iha ca padārthadvayaṃ nirddhāritam ātmānātmā ca. tatrānātmanas tāvan nājñānenabhisaṃbandhaḥ. tasya hi svarūpam evajñānaṃ; na hi svato'jñānasyājñānaṃ ghaṭate. saṃbhavad apy ajñānasvabhāve'jñānaṃ kam atiśayaṃ janayet? na ca tatra jñānaprāptir asti, yena tatpratiṣedhātmakam ajñānaṃ syāt. anātmanaś cājñāna prasūtatvāt. na hi pūrvasiddhaṃ sat tato labdhātma lābhasya setsyata āśrayaṣyāśrayi saṃbhavati. tad-anapekṣasya ca, tasya nissvabhāvatvāt. etebhya eva hetubhyo nānātma viṣayam ajñānaṃ saṃbhavatīti grāhyam. evaṃ tāvan nānātmano'jñānitvaṃ, nāpi tadviṣayam ajñānam. pāriśeṣyād ātmana evāstv ajñānaṃ, tasyājño'smity anubhava darśanāt. "so'haṃ bhagavo mantravid evāsmi nātmavit" iti śruteḥ. na cātmano'jñānasvarūpatā, tasya caitanyamātra svābhāvyād atiśayaś ca saṃbhavati jñānaviparilopo, jñāna prāpteś ca saṃbhavas, tasya jñānakāritvāt. na cājñāna kāryatvaṃ, kūṭasthātmasvābhāvyād ajñānānapekṣasya cātmanaḥ svata eva svarāpasiddher yuktam ātmana evājñā tvam. kiṃ viṣayaṃ punas tad ātmano'jñānam? ātmaviṣayam iti brūmaḥ. nanv ātmano'pi jñānasvarūpatvād, ananyatvāc ca, jñānaprakṛtivādibhyaś ca, hetubhyo naivajñānaṃ ghaṭate.

ghaṭata eva. katham? ajñānamātranimittatvāt tadvibhāgasya sarpātmateva rajjvāḥ. tasmāt tadapanuttau dvaitānarthābhāvaḥ. tadapanodaś ca vākyād eva tatpadapadārthābhijñasya. ato vākyavyākhyānāyādhyāya ārabhyate. tatra yathoktena prakāreṇa tattvamasyādivākyonpaniviṣṭapadapadārthayoḥ kṛtānvayavyatirekaḥ.

yadā nā tattvamasy āder brahmāsmīty avagacchati
pradhvastāh aṃ mamo naiti tadā gīrmanasoḥ sṛtim (1)

yadaiva tadarthaṃ tvamarthe'vaiti tadaivāvākyārthatāṃ pratipadyate gīrmanasoḥ sṛtiṃ na pratipadyata iti. kuta etad adhyavasīyate? yasmāt

tatpadaṃ prakṛtārthaṃ syāt tvaṃ-padam pratyagātmani
nīlotpalavad etābhyāṃduḥkhyanātmatvavāraṇe (2)

evaṃ kṛtānvayavyatireko vākyād evāvākyārthaṃ pratipadyata ity uktam atas tadvyākhyānāya sūtropanyāsaḥ

sāmānādhikaraṇyam ca viśeṣaṇaviśeṣyatā
lakṣyalakṣaṇasaṃbandhaḥ padārthapratyagātmanām (3)

asmin sūtra upanyaste kaścic codayati "yo'yaṃ vākyārthapratipattau pūrvādhyāyenānvayavyatirekalakṣaṇo nyāyaḥ sarvakarmasaṃnyāsapūrvako'bhihitaḥ, kiṃ ayaṃ vidhiparipräpitaḥ, kiṃ vā svarasata evātra pumān pravartata iti. kiṃcātaḥ? śṛṇu. yady ātmavastusākṣātkaraṇāya vidhiparipräpito'yaṃ nyāyas, tadā'vaśyam ātmavastusākṣātkaraṇāyavyāvṛttaśubhāśubhakarmarāśir. ekāgramanā, anvayavyatirekābhyāṃ yathoktābhyām ātmadarśanaṃ karoti. aparisamāpyātmadarśanaṃ tataḥ pracyavamāna ārūḍhapatito bhavati. yadi punar, yadṛcchātaḥ pravartate, tadā na kaścid doṣa" iti. vidhiparipräpita iti brūmo. yata āha

śamādisādhanaḥ paśyed ātmany ātmānam añjasā
anvayavyatirekābhyāṃ tyaktvā yuṣmad aśeṣataḥ (4)

yusmadarthe parityakte pūrvoktair hetubhiḥ śrutiḥ
vikṣāpannasya ko'smīti tat tvam ity āha sauhṛdāt (5)

atrāpi codayanti sāṃkhyāḥ. "śarīrendriyamanobuddhiṣv anātmasv, ātmeti nissaṃdhibandhanaṃ mithyājñānam-ajñānaṃ. tannibandhano hy ātmano'nekānarthasaṃbandhas tasya cānvayavyatirekābhyām eva nirastatvān, nirviṣayaṃ tattvamasyādivākyaṃ prāptam. tasmād vākyasya caiṣa mahimā yo'yam ātmānātmanor vibhāga" iti. tannirākaraṇā-yedam ucyate

bhedasaṃvid idaṃ jñānaṃ bhedābhāvaś ca sākṣiṇi
kāryam etad avidyāyā jñātmanā tyājayed vacaḥ (6)

jñātmanā tyājayed vaca ity upaśrutyāha kaścit. mithyā-jñānavyatirekeṇātmānavabodhasyābhāvāt kiṃ vākyena nivartyate? ajñāna hi nāma jñānābhāvas. tasya cāvastu-svābhāvyāt kutaḥ saṃsārakāraṇatvaṃ? na hy asataḥ saj-janmeṣyate "kutas tu khalu somyaivaṃ syāt" iti, "katham-asataḥ saj jāyeta" iti śruter iti. atrocyate

ajñāta eva sarvo'rthaḥ prāg yato buddhijanmanaḥ
ekenaiva satā saṃś ca sann ajñāto bhavet tataḥ (7)

sann ajñāto bhavet tata ity uktam adhastanena ślokena. ko'sau sann ajñāta ity apekṣāyāṃ tatsvarūpaprati-pādanāyāha

pramitsāyāṃ ya ābhāti svayaṃ mātṛpramāṇayoḥ
svamahimnā ca yas siddhaḥ so'jñātārtho'vasīyatām (8)

atra kecid āhuḥ. yatkiṃcid iha vākyaṃ laukikaṃ vaidikaṃ vā tat sarvaṃ saṃsargātmakam eva vākyārthaṃ gamayati. atas tattvamasyādivākyebhyaḥ saṃsargātmakam "ahaṃ brahma"iti vijñāya, tāvan nididhyāsīta yāvad avākyārthātmakaḥ pratyagātmaviṣayo'vabodhah "ahaṃ brahma" iti samabhijāyate. tasmād eva vijñānāt kaivalyam-āpnotīti. tannirākaraṇāyedam ucyate

sāmānādhikaraṇyāder ghaṭetarakhayor iva
vyāvṛtteḥ syād avākyārthaḥ sākṣān nas tattvamarthayoḥ (9)

kuto'vākyārtho'vasiyata iti cet, tatpratipattyarthaṃ viśeṣaṇaviśeṣyayoḥ sāmarthyoktiḥ

nirduḥkhitvaṃ tvamarthasya tadarthena viśeṣaṇāt
pratyaktā ca tadarthasya tvaṃpadenāsya saṃnidheḥ (10)

uktaṃ sāmānādhikaraṇyaṃ viśeṣaṇaviśeṣyabhāvaś ca saṃkṣepato'tha lakṣyalakṣaṇavyākhyānāyāha

kūṭasthabodhapratyaktvam animittaṃ sadātmanaḥ
boddhṛtāh aṃtayor hetus tābhyāṃ tenopalakṣyate (11)

buddheḥ kūṭasthabodhapratyaktvanimitte boddhṛtāpratyaktve ye tv asādhāraṇe, tayor viśeṣavacanam

boddhṛtā kartṛtā buddheḥ karmatā syād ahaṃtayā
tayor aikyaṃ yathā buddhau pūrvayor evam ātmani (12)

yathā buddhau pūrvayor evam ātmanīty atideśena buddhi-sādharmyavidhānān, nānātvaprasaktau tadapavādārtham-āha

dharmadharmitvabhedo'syāḥ so'pi naivātmano yataḥ
pratyagjyotir ato'bhinnaṃ bhedahetor asaṃbhavāt (13)

bhedahetvasaṃbhavaṃ darśayann āha

na kasyāṃcid avasthāyām bodhapratyaktvayor bhidā
vyabhicāro'thavā dṛṣṭo yathā'haṃtadvidos sadā (14)

yasmād ajñānopādānāyā eva buddher bhedo nātmanas, tasmād etat siddham

kūṭasthabodhato'dvaitaṃ sākṣāt tvaṃ pratyagātmanaḥ
kūṭasthabodhād boddhrī dhīḥ svato hīyaṃ vināśvarī (15)

athādhunā prakṛtasyaiva pariṇāminaḥ kūṭasthasya ca lakṣaṇam ucyate

viśeṣaṃ kaṃcid āśritya yat svarūpaṃ pratīyate
pratyabhijñāpramāṇena pariṇāmī sa dehavat (16)

sāmānyāc ca viśeṣāc ca svamahimnaiva yo bhavet
vyutthāyāpy avikāri syāt kumbhākāśādivat tu saḥ (17)

ātmano buddheś ca bodhapratyagātmatvam abhihitaṃ. tayor asādhāraṇalakṣaṇābhidhānārtham āha

buddher yat pratyagātmatvaṃ tat syād dehādyupāśrayāt
ātmanas tu svarūpaṃ tan nabhasaḥ suṣitā yathā (18)

boddhṛtvaṃ tadvad evāsyāḥ pratyayotpattihetutaḥ
ātmanas tu svarūpaṃ tat tiṣṭhantīva mahībhṛtaḥ (19)

tayoḥ kūṭasthapariṇāminor ātmānavabodha eva saṃbandha-hetur, na punar vāstavaḥ kaścid api saṃbandha upapadyata ity āha

samyaksaṃśayamithyātvair ddhīr eveyaṃ vibhajyate
hānopādānatā'mīśāṃ mohād adhyasyate dṛśau (20)

kutaḥ kūṭasthātmasiddhir iti ced, yataḥ

na hānaṃ hāna mātreṇa nodayo'piyatā yataḥ
tatsiddhiḥ syāt tu taddhīne hānādānavidharmake (21)

evam

āgamāpāyihetubhyāṃ dhūtvā sarvān anātmanaḥ
tatas tattvamasītyetadd hanty asmadi nijaṃ tamaḥ (22)

ityādi punaḥ punar ucyate granthalāghavād buddhi-lāghavaṃ prayojakamiti. tatra yadyapi tattvamasyādi-vākyād upāditsitādvitīyātmārthavat pārokṣyasadvitī-yārthaḥ pratīyate. tathāpi tu naivāsāv arthaḥ śrutyā tātparyeṇa pratipipādayiṣitaḥ, prāg apy etasya pratītatvād itīmam artham āha

tad ity etat padaṁ loke bahvarthapratipādakam
aparityajya pārokṣyam abhidhānottham eva tat (23)

tvam ity api padaṃ tadvat sākṣānmātrārtha vāci tu
saṃsāritām asaṃtyajya sāpi syād abhidhānajā (24)

viruddhoddeśanatvāc ca parokṣyaduḥkhitvayor avivakṣitatvam ity āha

uddhiśyamānaṃ vākyasthaṃ noddeśanaguṇānvitam
ākāṅkṣitapadārthena saṃsargaṃ pratipadyate (25)

yata etad evam, ato'nupāditsitayor api tattvamarthayorviśeṣaṇaviśeṣyabhāvo bhedasaṃsargarahitāvākyārthalakṣaṇāyaivety upasaṃhāraḥ

tado viśeṣaṇārthatvaṃ viśeṣyatvaṃ tvamas tathā
lakṣyalakṣaṇasaṃbandhas tayoḥ syāt pratyagātmanā (26)

kathaṃ punar avivakṣitaviruddhanirasyamānasya

lakṣaṇaṃ sarpavad rajjvāḥ praticaḥ syād ahaṃ tathā
tadbādhenaiva vākyārthaṃ vetti so'pi tadāśrayāt (27)

iyaṃ cā vākyārthapratipattir anvayavyatirekābhijñāsyaiva. yasmāt

yāvad yāvan nirasyāyaṃ dehādin pratyagañcati
tāvat tāvat tadartho'pi tvamarthaṃ pravivikṣati (28)

kasmāt punaḥ kārāṇād dehādyanātmatvapratipattāv evātmā tadarthamātmatvenābhiliṅgate, na viparyaya iti? ucyate. pratyagātmānavabodhasyānātmasvābhāvyāt, tadabhinir-vṛttaś cāyaṃ buddhyādidehāntas, tasminn ātmatvam avidyā-kṛtam evātmatvam ivānātmatvam api sāvidyasyaiva. yato niravidyo vidvān avākyārtharūpa eva kevalo'vaśiṣyate tasmād ucyate

dehādi vyavadhānatvāt tadarthaṃ svayam apy ataḥ
pārokṣyeṇaiva jānāti sākṣāttvaṃ tadanātmanaḥ (29)

yathoktārthapratipattisaukaryāya dṛṣṭāntopādānam

pratyag udbhūtapittasya yathā bāhyārthapītatā
caitanyaṃ pratyagātmīyaṃ bahir vad dṛśyate tathā (30)

yasmād evam, ato viśuddham avasīyatām

padāny uddhṛtya vākyebhyo hy anvayavyatirekataḥ
padārthāṃ llokato buddhvā vetti vākyārtham añjasā (31)

kutaḥ punaḥ sāmānyamātravṛtteḥ padasya vākyārtha-pratipattihetutvam iti? bāḍham

sāmānyaṃ hi padaṃ brūte viśeṣo vākyakartṛkaḥ
śrutyādipratibaddhaṃ sad viśeṣārthaṃ bhavet padam (32)

anvayavyatirekapurassaraṃ vākyam eva sāmānādhi-karaṇyādināvidyāpaṭalapradhvaṃsadvāreṇa mumukṣum svārājye'bhiṣecayati na tv anvayavyatirekamātrasādh-yo'yam artha ity āha

buddhyādīnām anātmatvaṃ liṅgād api ca sidhyati
nivṛttis tāvatā netīty ato vākyaṃ samāśrayet (33)

na kevalam anumānamātraśaraṇo'bhilaṣitam arthaṃ na prāpnotīty, anarthaṃ cāpnotīty āha

anādṛtya śrutiṃ mohād ato bauddhās tamasvinaḥ
āpedire nirātmatvam anumānaikacakṣuṣaḥ (34)

na cānādare kāraṇam asti. yasmāt sarvatraivānādaranimittaṃ pramāṇasya pramāṇāntarapratipannapratipādanaṃ vā, viparītapratipādanaṃ vā, saṃśayitapratipādanaṃ vā, na vā pratipādanam iti. na caiteṣām anyatamad api kāraṇam asti. yata āha

mānāntarānavaṣṭabdhaṃ nirduḥkhyātmānam añjasā
bodhayantī śrutiḥ kena na pramāṇam itīryate (35)

na ca saṃśayitavyam avagamayati. yataḥ

sarvasaṃśayahetau hi niraste katham ātmani
jāyeta saṃśayo vākyād anumānena yuṣmadi (36)

api ca

yatra syāt saṃśayo nāsau jñeya ātmeti paṇḍitaiḥ
na yataḥ saṃśayaprāptir ātmano'vagatitvataḥ (37)

anavabodhakatvaṃ tu dūrotsāritam eva. yata āha

bodhye'py anubhavo yasya na kathaṃcana jāyate
taṃ kathaṃ bodhayec chāstraṃ loṣṭaṃ narasamākṛtim (38)

anvayavyatirekapurassaraṃ vākyam evāvākyārtharūpam ātmānaṃ pratipādayatīty asya pakṣasya draḍhimne śrutyudāharaṇam upanyasyati

jighrāṇīmam ahaṃ gandham iti yo vetty avikriyaḥ
sa ātmā tat paraṃ jyotiḥ śirasīdaṃ vacaḥ śruteḥ (39)

yathā "tat satyaṃ sa ātmā tattvamasi" ity asya śeṣatvenānvayavyatirekaśrutir yathā "ya eṣo'kṣiṇi puruṣo dṛśyate" ity ādyā "atha yo vededaṃ jighrāṇi" ity antā. tathā "ahaṃ brahmāsmi" ity asya śeṣaḥ

ahamaḥ pratyagātmārtho nirastāśeṣayuṣmadaḥ
bambhaṇīti śrutir nyāyyā yo'yam ity ādinā'sakṛt (40)

kathaṃ punar ayam artho'vasīyate ahaṃvyājenātrātmārtho bubodhayiṣita iti? yataḥ

eṣa ātmā svayaṃjyotī ravisomāgnivākṣu saḥ
iteṣv astaṃ dṛg evāste bhāsayaṃś cittaceṣṭitam (41)

nirṇenekti ca pṛṣṭo muniḥ

ātmanaivety upaśrutya ko'yam ātmety udīrite
buddheḥ paraṃ svato muktam ātmānaṃ munir abhyadhāt (42)

yasmāc cātmātrāhaṃvyājena pratyaṅmātro jigrāhayiṣitas, tasmād ahaṃvṛttiḥ svarūpasya vilayenaiva vākyārthāvagamāya kāraṇatvaṃ pratipadyata itīmam artham āha

ahaṃvṛttyaiva tad brahma yasmād eṣo'vagacchati
tatsvarūpalayenātaḥ kāraṇaṃ syād ahaṃkṛtiḥ (43)

ata eva ca yaḥ pratijñāto'rtho "nāhaṃgrāhye na taddhīne" ityādiḥ, sa yuktibhir upapādita iti kṛtvopasaṃhriyate

gṛhītahaṃpadārthaś cet kasmāj jño na prapadyate
pratyakṣādivirodhāc cet pratīcy uktir na yuṣmadi (44)

pūrvasyaiva ślokārthasya vispaṣṭārtham āha

parāñcy eva tu sarvāṇi pratyakṣādini nātmani
pratīcy eva pravṛttam tat sad asīti vaco'ñjasā (45)

tasmāt pramātṛpramāṇaprameyebhyo hīyamānopādīyamānebhyo'nvayavyatirekābhyāṃ muñjeṣīkāvad aśeṣabuddhivikriyāsākṣitayātmānaṃ niṣkṛṣya, tattvamasyādivākyebhyo'pūrvādilakṣaṇam ātmānaṃ vijānīyāt. tad etad āha

ahaṃduḥkhī sukhī ceti yenāyaṃ pratyayo'dhruvaḥ
avagatyanta ābhāti sa ma ātmeti vākyadhīḥ (46)

pramāṇāntarānavaṣṭabdhaṃ nirastāśeṣakāryakāraṇātmakadvaitaprapañcaṃ satyajñānānandalakṣaṇam ātmānaṃ "tattvamasy", "ahaṃ-brahmāsmi", ity ādivākyaṃ saṃśayitamithyājñānājñānapradhvaṃsamukhena sākṣādaparokṣāt karatalanyastāmalakavat pratipādayaty evety asakṛdabhihitam. tatra kecidāhuḥ 'tattvamasyādivākyair yathāvasthitavastuyāthātmyānvākhyānaniṣṭhair, na yathokto'rthaḥ pratipattum śakyate, 'bhidhāśrutitvāt teṣām. na hi loke'bhidhāśruteḥ pramāṇāntaranirapekṣāyā "nadyās tīre phalāni santi", ityādikāyāḥ pramāṇyam abhyupagatam. ato niyogamukhenaivābhidhāśruteḥ pramāṇyaṃ yuktaṃ pramāṇāntaranirapekṣatvān niyogasya.' asya parihārārtham aśeṣapratyakṣādiprameyatvanirākaraṇadvāreṇ ātīndriyārthaviṣayatvād abhidhāśruteḥ prāmāṇyaṃ suptapuruṣaprabodhakavākyasyeva vaktavyam ity ayam ārambhaḥ

nityāvagatirūpatvād anyamānānapekṣaṇāt
śabdādiguṇahīnatvāt saṃśayānavatārataḥ (47)

tṛṣṇāniṣṭhīvanair nātmā pratyakṣādyaiḥ pramīyate
pratyagātmatvahetoś ca svārthatvād aprameyataḥ (48)

śrutir apīmam arthaṃ nirvadati

didṛkṣitaparicchinnaparāgrūpādi saṃśrayāt
viparātam ato dṛṣṭyā svato buddhaṃ na paśyati (49)

nyāyasiddham ato vakti dṛṣṭer draṣṭārām ātmanaḥ
na paśyet pratyagātmānaṃ pramāṇaṃ śrutir ādarāt (50)

anumānāviṣayatve'nyad api kāraṇam ucyate

pratyakṣasya parāktvān na saṃbandhagrahaṇaṃ yataḥ
ātmano'to'numityāsyānubhavo na kathaṃcana (51)

evam ayaṃ pramātṛpramāṇaprameyavyavahāraḥ sarva eva parācīnaviṣaya eva na pratīcīnam ātmānam avagāhayitum alam. evaṃ ca saty, anenaiva yathokto'rtho'vasātuṃ śakyata ity āha

pramāṇavyavahāro'yaṃ sarva eva parāg yataḥ
suvicāryāpy ato'nena yuṣmady eva didṛkṣate (52)

yasmāt laukika pratyakṣādipramanāṇādhigamyo'ham brahmāsmīti vākyārthas tasmāt

anvayavyatirekābhyāṃ nirasyāprāṇato yataḥ
vikṣāpannasya ko'smīti tad asīti śrutir jagau (53)

so'yam, anvayavyatirekanyāya etāvān eva yadavasāno vākyārthas tadabhijñasya "ahaṃ brahmāsmi", ity āvirbhavati. draṣṭṛdṛśyavibhāgenāgamāpāyisākṣivibhāgena ca śrutyabhyupagamataḥ saṃkṣipyocyate

dṛśyatvād ghaṭavad deho dehavac cendriyāṇy api
manaś cendriyavaj jñeyaṃ manovan niścayādimat (54)

tathā sakalakāryakāraṇāgamāpāyivibhāgasākṣitvenāpi

prāg asad yāti paścāt sat sac ca yāyād asat tathā
anātmābhijanaṃ tat syād viparītaḥ svayaṃ dṛśiḥ (55)

tatra ghaṭādināṃ dṛśyānām anātmatvaṃ draṣṭrātmapūrvakaṃ pratyakṣeṇaiva pramāṇenopalabhyānātmanaś cāsādhāraṇān dharmān avadhārya, tair dṛśyatvāgamāpāyādibhir dharmaiḥ śarīrendriyamanoniścayādivṛttīr anātmatayā vyudasyāhaṃvṛttimato'pi dṛśyatvāviśeṣād draṣṭṛpūrvakatvam avasīyate. tad etad āha

ghaṭādayo yathā liṅgaṃ syuḥ paramparayā'hamaḥ
dṛśyatvād ahaṃ apy evaṃ liṅgaṃ syād draṣṭur ātmanaḥ (56)

nanu draṣṭṛdarśanadṛśyānāṃ jāgratsvapnasuṣupteṣv, āgamāpāyadarśanād yat sākṣīkau teṣāmāgamāpāyau, sa āgamāpāyavibhāgarahita ātmā yathā yannibandhanau jagataḥ prakāśāprakāśau, sa prakāśāprakāśavibhāgarahitaḥ sūrya iti. yadā caivam, tadā vākyāvagamyasyārthasyānuditānastamitavijñānamātrasvabhāvasyānumānenaiva pratipannatvāt punar api vākyasya nirviṣayatvaprasaṅgaḥ. naiṣa doṣaḥ. liṅgavyavadhānena tatpratipatteḥ. nanu sākṣādaparokṣādātmasvabhāvenānātmano hānopādānayoḥ saṃbandhagrahaṇāt, kam atiśayaṃ vākyaṃ kuryāt? maivam vocaḥ. liṅgādhīnatvāt tatpratipatteḥ. na hi liṅgavyavadhānenātmapratipattiḥ sākṣātpratipattir bhavati, "yam evaiṣa vṛṇute tena labhyaḥ" iti śruteḥ. ata āha

liṅgam astitvaniṣṭhatvān na syād vākyārthabodhakam
sadasadvyutthitātmā'yam ato vākyāt pratīyate (57)

nanu yadi vyāvṛttasadasadvikalpajālaṃ vastv abhīṣṭaṃ vākyād bhavatas, tathāpi tūtsāryate vākyaviṣayā tṛṣṇā. yasmād antareṇāpi vākyaśravaṇaṃ nirastāśeṣavikalpam āgopālāvipālapaṇḍitaṃ suṣupte vastu siddham, ato nārtho vākyaśravaṇena. naitad evam. kiṃ kāraṇam? sarvānarthabījasyātmānavabodhasya suṣupte saṃbhavāt. yadi hi suṣupte'jñānaṃ nābhaviṣyad, antareṇāpi vedāntavākyaśravaṇamanananididhyāsanāny "ahaṃ brahmāsmi" ityadhyavasāyāt sarvaprāṇabhṛtāmapi svarasata eva suṣuptapratipatteḥ sakalasaṃsārocchittiprasaṅgaḥ. na ca kaivalyāt punarutthānaṃ nyāyyam, anirmokṣaprasaṅgāt. na ca "anya eva suṣupto'nya evotthita" iti śakyaṃ vaktuṃ, "nādrākṣamahaṃ suṣupte'nyat kiṃcidapi" ityutthitasya pratyabhijñādarśanāt. tasmād, avaśyaṃ suṣupte'jñānamabhyupagantavyam. nanu yadi tatrājñānam abhaviṣyad, rāgadveṣaghaṭājñānādivat pratyakṣam abhaviṣyad, yatheha loke "ghaṭaṃ na jānāmi" ity ajñānam avyavahitaṃ pratyakṣam. atrocyate. na. abhivyañjakābhāvāt. katham abhivyañjakābhāva iti cecchṛṇu

bāhyāṃ vṛttim anutpādya vyaktiḥ syān nāhamo yathā
narte'ntaḥkaraṇaṃ tadvad dhvāntasya vyaktir āñjasī (58)

kaścid atikrāntaṃ pratismṛtya "dṛśyatvād aham apy evaṃ liṅgaṃ syād draṣṭur ātmanaḥ" iti niryuktikam abhihitam ityāha. kiṃ kāraṇam? ahaṃtajjñātror vivekāprasiddheḥ. yatheha ghaṭadevadattayor grāhyagrāhakatvena sphuṭataro vibhāgaḥ prasiddho loke, na tathehāhaṃkāratajjñātror vibhāgo'stīti. tasmād, asādhv etad abhihitam iti. atrocyate

dāhyadāhakataikatra yatha syād vahnidāruṇoḥ
jñeyajñātṛkataivaṃ syād ahaṃjñātroḥ parasparam (59)

evaṃ tāvad avidyotthasyāntaḥkaraṇasya bāhyaviṣaya-nimittarūpāvacchedāyāhaṃvṛttir vyāpriyate. tayāvacchinnaṃ sat kūṭasthapratyagātmopādānāvabodharūpasyāvyavadhānatayā viṣayabhāvaṃ pratipadyata iti. tatra tayor jñātrahaṃtārūpayor avabhāsakāvabhāsyatvasaṃbandhavyatirekeṇa nānyat saṃbandhāntaram upapadyate. ahaṃtārūpaṃ tv ātmasātkṛtvā'haṃkañcukaṃ paridhāyopakāryatvopakārakatvakṣamaḥ san, bāhyaviṣayeṇopakāriṇāpakāriṇā v ātmātmīyaṃ saṃbandhaṃ pratipadyate. tadabhidhīyate

idaṃ jñānaṃ bhavej jñātur mamajñānaṃ tathāhamaḥ
ajñānopādhinedaṃ syād vikriyāto'hamo mama (60)

ekasyaiva jñātur, antarbāhyanimittabhedād vibhinne'pi viṣaya "idaṃ" "mama" iti jñānaṃ dvairūpyaṃ jāyata ityuktam. atropakriyamāṇāpakriyamāṇasyaiva jñātur viṣaye mamapratyayo bhavati. viparyaye cedaṃpratyaya iti katham avagamyate? avagamyatām anvayavyatirekābhyām. tat katham ity āha

anupakriyamāṇatvān na jñātuḥ syād ahaṃ mama
ghaṭādivad idaṃ tu syān mohamātravyapāśrayāt (61)

mohatatkāryāśrayatvāj jñātṛtvavikriyayoḥ pūrvatredaṃmamajñānānvayaḥ pradariśtaḥ. athādhunā tadvyatirekeṇa vyatirekapradarśanārtham āha

vikriyājñānaśūnyatvān nedaṃ na ca mamātmanaḥ
utthitasya sato'jñānam nāham ajñāsiṣaṃ yataḥ (62)

ātmānātmavivekasyeyattāpradarśanārtham āha

vākyapratyakṣamānābhyām iyān arthaḥ pratīyate
anarthakṛttamohānir vākyād eva sadātmanaḥ (63)

dvitīyādhyāyādau śrotṛcatuṣṭayam upanyastam. tatra kṛtsnānātmanivṛttau satyāṃ yaḥ pratyagātmany avākyārthatāṃ pratipadyate, sa kṣapitāśeṣāntarāyahetur iti, na taṃ prati vaktavyaṃ kiṃcid apy avaśiṣyate. yo'pi vākyaśravaṇamātrād eva pratipadyate, tasyāpy atīndriyaśaktimattvān na kiṃcid apy apekṣitavyam asti. yaś ca śrāvita-tattvamasyādivākyaḥ svayam evānvayavyatirekau kṛtvā, tad-avasāna eva vākyārthaṃ pratipadyate'sāv api yathārthaṃ pratipanna iti pūrvavad evopekṣitavyaḥ. yaḥ punar anvaya-vyatirekau kārayitvāpi punaḥ punar vākyaṃ śrāvyate yathābhūtārthapratipattaye, tasya kṛtānvaya-vyatirekasya sataḥ kathaṃ vākyaṃ śrāvyata iti? ucyate

navasaṃkhyāhṛtajñāno daśamo vibhramād yathā
na vetti daśamo'smīti vīkṣamāṇo'pi tān nava (64)

atha dṛṣṭāntagatam arthaṃ dārṣṭāntikārthe samarpayiṣyann āha

apaviddhadvayo'py evaṃ tattvamasyādinā vinā
vetti naikalam ātmānaṃ nānveṣyaṃ cātra kāraṇam (65)

"nānveṣyaṃ cātra kāraṇam ity uktaṃ, tat kasmād?" iti codite pratyāhānveṣaṇāsahiṣṇutvāt. "tat katham ity?" āha

seyaṃ bhrāntir nirālambā sarvanyāyavirodhinī
sahate na vicāraṃ sā tamo yadvad divākaram (66)

tasyāḥ khalv asyā avidyāyā bhrānteḥ samyagjñānotpatti-dvāreṇa nivṛttiḥ

bubhutsocchedinī cāsya sad asityādinā dṛḍham
pratīci pratipattiḥ syān nāsau mānāntarād bhavet (67)

katham punar vākyam pratipādayaty eveti ced, dṛṣṭāntoktiḥ

jijñāsor daśamaṃ yadvan navātikramya tāmyataḥ
tvam eva daśamo'sīti kuryād evaṃ pramāṃ vacaḥ (68)

sa ca tattvamasyādivākyaśravaṇajā pramotpannatvād eva. na ca naivam iti pratyayāntaraṃ jāyate. tad etad dṛṣṭāntena pratipādayati

daśamo'sīti vākyotthā na dhīrasya vihanyate
ādimadhyāvasāneṣu na navasv asya saṃśayaḥ (69)

evaṃ tat tvam asīty asmād dvaitanut pratyagātmani
samyagjñātatvam arthasya jāyetaiva pramā dṛḍhā (70)

pratyagātmani pramopajāyata ity uktaṃ tatra codyate. "kiṃ yathāghaṭādiprameyaviṣayā pramā kartrādikārakabhedā-napahnavena jāyate tathaivotāśeṣakārakagrāmopamardena kartuḥ pratyagātmani?" iti. ucyate

pratyaktā'sya svato rūpaṃ niṣkriyākārakāphalam
advitīyaṃ tadiddhā dhīḥ pratyagātmeva lakṣyate (71)

yadmād evam

vipaścito'py atas tasyām ātmabhāvaṃ vitanvate
davīyass vindriyārtheṣu kṣīyate hy uttarottaram (72)

āha. yadi vākyam eva yathābhūtārthāvabodhakam, atha kasya hetor avidyotthāpitasya kartṛtvāder upadeśa ity? ukte pratividhīyate

bhrāntiprasiddhyā'nūdyārtham tat tattvaṃ bhrāntibādhayā
ayaṃ nety upadiśyeta tathaivaṃ tat tvam ityapi (73)

imam arthaṃ dṛṣṭāntena buddhāv ārohayati

sthāṇuḥ sthāṇur itivoktir na nṛbuddhiṃ nirasyati
vyānuvādāt tathaivoktir bhrāntiṃpuṃso na bādhate (74)

yasmāc chrotṛprasiddhānuvādy eva tvam iti padaṃ, tasmād uddiśyamāna sthatvād duḥkhitvāder avivakṣitatvam eva. vidhīyamānatve hi sati virodhaprasaṅgo, na tu vidhīyamānānūdyamānayor iti. svapradhānayor hi padayor virodhāśaṅkā sāmānyāl iṅgitatvāt tayor na viparyaye

anāl iṅgitasāmānyau na jihāsitavādinau
vyutthitau tattvamau tasmād anyonyābhisamīkṣaṇau (75)

apāstasāmānyārthatvād, anuvādasthatvād, vidhīyamānena ca saha virodhād, duḥkhitvāder astu kāmaṃ jihāsitārthayor asaṃsargo yathopanyastadoṣavirahāt, tattvamarthayoḥ saṃsargo'stu nīlotppalavad iti cen, naivam apy upapadyate. yasmāt

tadarthayos tu niṣṭhātmā dvayapārokṣyavarjitaḥ
nādvitīyaṃ vinātmānaṃ nātmā nitya dṛśā vinā (76)

atrāha. "kiniha jihāsitaṃ, kiṃ vopāditisam?" iti. ucyate. pratyagātmārthābhidhāyinas tvapadād, ubhayaṃ pratīyate "ahaṃ duḥkhī", "pratyagātama" ca. tatra ca pratyagātmano'haṃ duḥkhīty anenābhisaṃbandha ātmayāthātmy-ānavabodhahetuka eva. ato'hamartho'narthopasṛṣṭatvād, ajñānottohatvāc ca heya iti pratyakṣatovasīyate. "tadarthe kiṃ heyaṃ, kiṃ vopādeyam iti nāvadhriyate." tata idam abhidhīyate.

pārokṣyaṃ yat tadarthe syāt tadd heyam ahamarthavat
pratīcevāhamo'bhedaḥ pārokṣyeṇātmano'pi me (77)

"kathaṃ punas tadartho'dvitīyalakṣaṇaḥ pratyag-ātmopāśrayaṃ sadvitīyatvaṃ duḥkhitvaṃ niranvayam apamudatīti? ucyate. na caitayor nivartakanivartyabhāvaṃ vayaṃ brūmaḥ. kathaṃ tarhi? tvamarthe pratyagātmani prāganavabuddhādvitīyatā sānenāvabodhyate. ato'nava-bodhanirāsena tadutthasya sadvītiyatvasya tvamartha-sthasya, parokṣatvasya ca tadarthasthasya nirasanān, na vaiyadhikaraṇyādicodyasyāvasaro'stīti. tad idam abhi-dhīyate.

tat tvamarthena saṃpṛtoko nānātvaṃ vinivartayet
nāparityaktapārokṣyam tvaṃ tadarthaṃ sisṛpsati (78)

"kasmāt punaḥ kāraṇāt tadartho'dvitīyalakṣaṇas tvam-arthena pratyagātmanā apṛthagarthaḥ sann avidyottham sa-dvitīyatvaṃ nihantīti?" ucyate. virodhāt. tad ucyate.

saṃsāritādvitīyena pārokṣyam cātmanā saha
prāsaṅgikaṃ viruddhatvāt tattvambhyāṃ bādhanaṃ tayoḥ.
(79)

tattvamarthayos tu bādhakatve' nyadapi kāraṇam ucyate

ajñātapuruṣārthatvāc chrautatvāt tattvamarthayoḥ
svam artham aparitiyajya bādhakau stāṃ viruddhayoḥ (80)

evaṃ tāvad yathopakrāntena prakriyāvartmanā na pratyakṣādipramāṇāntarair virodhagandho'pi saṃbhāvyate. yadā punaḥ sarvaprakāreṇāpi yatamānā naivemaṃ vākyārthaṃ saṃbhāvayāmaḥ, pratyakṣādipramāṇāntara-virodhata eva, tasminn api pakṣa ucyate.

pratyakṣādiviruddhaṃ ced vākyam arthaṃ vadet kvacit
syāt tu taddṛṣṭividhyarthaṃ yoṣāgnivadasaṃśayam (81)

yadā tu tattvamasyādi vākyaṃ sarvaprakāreṇāpi vicāryamāṇaṃ na kriyāṃ kaṭākṣeṇāpi vikṣate, tadā prasaṃkhyānādi vyāpāro dussaṃbhāvya iti. tad ucayate

vastvekaniṣṭhaṃ vākyaṃ cen na tasya syāt kriyārthatā
vastuno hy ekarūpatvād vikalasyāpy asaṃbhavaḥ (82)

bhinnaviṣayatvāc ca na pramāṇāntaravirodhaḥ katham? ucyate

apūrvādhigamaṃ kurvat pramāṇaṃ syān na cen na tat
na virodhas tato yukto vibhinnārthāvabodhinoḥ (83)

ya evam api bhinnaviṣayāṇāṃ virodhaṃ vakti, so'trāpi virodhaṃ brūyāt

nāyaṃ śabdaḥ kuto yasmād rūpaṃ paśyāmi cakṣuṣā
iti yadvat tathaivāyaṃ virodho'kṣajavākyayoḥ (84)

pramāṇānāṃ satāṃ na virodhaḥ śrottrādīnām iva bhinna-viṣayatvāt. yayoś cābhinnaviṣyatvaṃ tayor ākhunakulayor iva pratiniyata eva bādhyabādhakabhāvaḥ syāt. atas tad ucyate

pratyakṣaṃ cen na śābdaṃ syāc chābdaṃ ced akṣajaṃ katham
pratyakṣābhāsaḥ pratyakṣe hy āgamābhāsa āgame (85)

na ca pratijñāhetudṛṣṭāntanyāya iha saṃbhavati, śabdādīnāṃ pratyekaṃ pramāṇatvād ata āha

svamahimnā pramāṇāni kurvaty arthāvabodhanam
itaretarasācivye prāmāṇyaṃ neṣyate svataḥ (86)

na ca sukhaduḥkhādisaṃbandho'vagatyātmanaḥ pratyakṣādipramāṇair gṛhyate, yena virodhaḥ pratyakṣādhipramāṇair udbhāvyate. katham? śṛṇu

duḥkhitāvagatau cet syān na pramīyeta sātmavat
karmaṇy eva pramā nyāyyā na tu kartary api kvacit (87)

abhyupagame'pi ca prasaṃkhyānaśatenāpi naiva tvaṃ saṃbhāvitadoṣān mucyase. ata āha

pramāṇabaddhamūlatvād duḥkhitvaṃ kena vāryate
agnyuṣṇavannivṛttiś cen nairātmyaṃ hy eti saugatam (88)

atha matam

nirākuryāt prasaṃkhyānaṃ duḥkhitvaṃ cet svanuṣṭhitam
pratyakṣādiviruddhatvāt katham utpādayet pramām (89)

nanu "prasaṃkhyānaṃ nāma tattvamasyādiśabdārthānvayavyatirekayuktiviṣayabuddhyāmreḍanam abhidhīyate. taccānuṣṭhīyamānanaṃ pramitivardhanayā paripūrṇāṃ pramitiṃ janajati, na punar aikāgrya-vardhanayeti, yathā'śeṣāśuciniḍe strīkuṇape kāminīti nirvastukaḥ puruṣāyāsamātrajanitaḥ pratyaya iti." tan na yataḥ

abhyāsopacayād buddher yat syād aikāgryam eva tat
na hi pramāṇāny abhyāsāt kurvanty arthāvadbodhanam (90)

abhyāsopacitā kṛtsnaṃ bhāvanā cen nivartayet
naikāntiki nivṛttis syād bhāvanājaṃ hi tatphalam (91)

api cāha

duḥkhy asmīty api ced dhvastā kalpakoṭyupabṛṃhiā
svalpīyo'bhyāsajā sthāsnvī bhāvanety atra kā pramā (92)

nanu śāstrāt sthāsnutvaṃ bhaiṣyati. naivam. yathāvasthita-vastuyāthātmyāvabobhamātrakāritvāc chāstrasya. na hi padārthaśaktyādhānakṛc chāstram. prasiddhaṃ. ca loke.

bhāvanājaṃ phalaṃ yat syād yac ca syāt karmaṇaḥ phalam
na tat sthāsnv iti mantavyaṃ draviḍeṣv iva saṅgatam (93)

yadapi pratyakṣādipramāṇopātta, ātmano duḥkhitvam. tathāpi tattvamasyādivākyotthapratyaya eva balīyān iti niścaya'vyabhicāriprāmāṇyavākyopāttatvāt prameyasya ca svata eva nirduḥkhitvasiddheḥ. pratyakṣādes tu savyabhicāritvāt saṃbhāvanāyāś ca puruṣaparikalpa-nāmātrāvaṣṭambhatvāc ceti.

nirduḥkhitvaṃ svatassiddhaṃ pratyakṣādeś ca duḥkhitā
ko hy ātmānam anādṛtya viśvased bāhyamāntaḥ (94)

saṃbandhārtha eva

api pratyakṣabādhena pravṛttiḥ pratyagātmani
"parāñci khānī" 'ty etasmād vacaso gamyate śruteḥ (95)

abhyupagamyaivam ucyate na tu pramaṇaṃ satpramāṇātareṇa virudhyata ity asakṛd avocāma. yatrāpi vākyapratyakṣayor virodhāśaṅkā tatrāpi puruṣamohavaśād eva sā jāyate na tu paramārthata iti. ata āha

pramāṃ cej janayed vākyaṃ pratyakṣādivirodhinīm
gauṇīṃ pratyakṣatāṃ brūyān mukhyārthāsaṃbhavād
budhaḥ (96)

tasyārthasya sukhapratipattyartham udāharaṇam

agnis samyag adhīte 'sau jahāsoccaiś ca mañcakaḥ
yathā tadvad ahaṃvṛttyā lakṣyate 'narhayāpi saḥ (97)

kasmāt punaḥ kāraṇāt sākṣād evātmā nābhidhīyate kim anayā kalpanayeti tatrāha

tvam ity etad vihāyānyam na vartmātmāvabodhane
samastīhas tvamartho'pi guṇaleśena vartate (98)

kasmāt punar hetor hy aham ity etad api guṇaleśena vartate na punaḥ sākṣād eveti. vidhūtasarvakalpanākāraṇa-svābhāvyād ātmanaḥ. ata āha

vyomni dhūmatuṣārābhramalinānīva durdhiyaḥ
kalpayeus tathāmūḍhāḥ saṃsāraṃ pratyagātmani (99)

nanu sarvakalpanānām apy ātmany atyantāsaṃbhave samāne 'haṃvṛttau kaḥ pakṣapāte hetur yena vṛttyantarāṇi vidhūyāhaṃvṛttyaivātmopalakṣyata iti. ucyate

cinnibheyam ahaṃvṛttiḥ pratīcīvātmano 'nyataḥ
pūrvoktebhyaś ca hetubhyas tasmād ātmānayocyate (100)

vṛttibhir yuṣmadarthābhir lakṣyate ced dṛśiḥ paraḥ
anātmatvaṃ bhavet tasya vitathaṃ ca vacaḥ śruteḥ (101)

yathoktena

anena guṇaleśena hy atyahaṃkartṛkarmayā
lakṣyate 'sāv ahaṃvṛttyā nāñjasātrābhidhīyate (102)

nāñjasātrābhidhīyata iti ko hetur iti cet

ṣaṣṭhīguṇakriyājātirūḍhayaḥ śabdahetavaḥ
nātmany anyatamo 'mīṣāṃ tenātmā nābhidhīyate (103)

yadi śabdo 'bhidhānābhidheyatvasaṃbandhāṅgīkāreṇa nātmani vartate kathaṃ śabdād ahaṃ brahmāsmīti samyagbodhotpattiḥ. ucyate

asatye vartmani sthitvā nirupāyam upeyate
ātmatvakāraṇād vidmo guṇavṛttyā vibodhitāḥ (104)

kathaṃ punar abhidhānam abhidheyenānabhisaṃbaddhaṃ sad anabhidheye 'rthe pramāṃ janayatīti śṛṇu yathānabhisaṃbaddham apy anabhidheye 'rthe 'vidyānirākaraṇamukhena bodhayatīty āha

śayānāḥ prāyaśo loke bodhyamānāḥ svanāmabhiḥ
sahasaiva prabudhyante yathaivaṃ pratyagātmani (105)

na hi nāmnāsti saṃbandho vyutthitasya śarīrataḥ
tathāpi budhyate tena yathaivaṃ tat tvam ity ataḥ (106)

yathā ca

bodhābodhau nabho 'spṛṣṭvā kṛṣṇadhīnīḍagau yathā
bādhyetarātmakau syātāṃ tathehātmani gamyatām (107)

"asatye vartmani sthitvā" ity upaśrutyātivismito mahatā saṃbhrameṇa kaścic codayati

nāsann upāyo loke 'sti paramārthaviniścaye
nāsalliṅgādd hi bāṣpadeḥ kaścid agniṃ prapadyate (108)

ity evaṃ codayed yo 'pi joṣayet taṃ ghaṭādinā sadasadbhyāṃ
vibhakto 'sau paryāyaś ca na cānayoḥ (109)

evaṃ kucodyam unmūlyāthedānīṃ prakṛtaṃ abhidhīyate. prakṛtaṃ cānabhidheye katham abhidhāśrutir avidyādhvaṃsy ātmani jñānaṃ janayatīti. tatraiva kāraṇāntaram ucyate

atidussṭho 'prabodho 'tra hanudity ātmaivāsya prabuddhatā
nimittamātrād vyety eṣā nāsāgre badaraṃ yathā (110)

anuditānastamitakūṭasthabodhamātrasvābhāvyād ātmano dussaṃbhāvyo 'vidyāsadbhāva iti cen na. avidyāprasiddhyaiva tatsadbhāvasiddher ulūkaniśāvad ity ata idam ucyate

aho dhārṣṭyam avidyāyā na kaścid ativartate
pramāṇaṃ vastv anādṛtya paramātmeva tiṣṭhati (111)

yasmād avidyāprasiddhyaivāvidyāsadbhāvasiddhir ata ātmavastuvṛttānurodhena na kathaṃcanāpi tatsaṃbhāvanāpy asti yata āha

jñānaṃ yasya nijaṃrūpaṃ kriyākārakavarjitam
saṃbhāvanāpy avidyāyās tatra syāt kena hetunā (112)

so 'yam evam anuditānastamitāvagatimātraśarīra ātmāpi sann avicāritaprasiddhāvidyāmātravyavahita evātathaivekṣyate yato 'taḥ

anumānād ayaṃ bhāvād vyāvṛtto 'bhāvam āśritaḥ
tato 'py asya nivṛttiḥ syād vākyād eva bubhitsataḥ (113)

bhāvavad abhāvād api nivṛttir anumānād eva kim iti na bhavatīti cec chṛṇu

na vyāvṛttir yathā yathā bhāvād bhāvenaivāviśeṣataḥ
abhāvād apy abhāvatvād vyāvṛttir na tatheṣyate (114)

yato nāunmānena vyāviddhāśeṣakriyākārakaphalātmani svārājye 'bhiṣektuṃ śakyate tasmāt

avidyānidrayā so 'yaṃ prasupto durvivekayā
bhāvābhāvavvyudāsinyā śrutyaiva pratibodhyate (115)

atrāh ānuditānastamitavijñānātmamātrasvarūpatvād dussaṃbhāvyā vidyeti. naitad evam. kutaḥ. yata āha

kuto 'vidyeti codyaṃ syān naiva prāgg hetvasaṃbhavāt
kālatrayāparicchitter na cordhvaṃ codyasaṃbhavaḥ (116)

yasmāt tattvamasyādivākyam evātmano 'śeṣām avidyāṃ niranvayām apanudati tasmāt

addhātamam anādṛtya pramāṇaṃ sad asīti ye
bubhutsante 'nyataḥ kuryus te 'kṣṇāpi rasavedanam (117)

evam apratihatām ahaṃ brahmeti pramāṃ tattvamasyādivākyaṃ kurvad api na pratipādayatīti ced abhimataṃ na kutaścanāpi pratipattiḥ syād ata āha

idaṃ ced anṛtaṃ brūyāt satyām avagatāv api
na cānyatrāpi viśvāso hy avagatyaviśeṣataḥ (118)

na copāditsitād vākyārthād vākyārthāntaraṃ kalpayituṃ yuktam. yasmāt

na ced anubhavo 'taḥ syāt padārthāvagatāv api
kalpyaṃ vidhyantaraṃ tatra na hy anyo 'rtho
'vagamyate (119)

na ca yathābhimato 'rtho yathoktena nyāyena nāvai
yate. ko 'sau nyāya ity āha

nāmādibhyo nirākṛtya tvamarthaṃ niṣparigrahaḥ
nisspṛho yuṣmadarthebhyaḥ śamādividhicoditaḥ (120)

bhaṅktvā cānnamayādiṃs tān pañcānātmatayā 'rgalān
ahaṃ brahmeti vākyārthaṃ vetti cen nārtha īhayā (121)

na ced evam upagamyate vākyasya pramāṇasya sato 'prāmāṇyaṃ prāpnoti. tad āha

yadarthaṃ ca pravṛttaṃ yad vākyaṃ tatra na cec chrutam
pramām utpādayet tasya prāmāṇyaṃ kena hetunā (122)

atha manyase

jānīyāc cet prasaṃkhyānāc chabdas satyavacāḥ katham
pārokṣyaṃ śabdo naḥ prāha prasaṃkhyānāt tv
asaṃśayam (123)

na ca yuktiśabdāvṛttilakṣaṇāt prasaṃkhyānād yathāvat pratipattir bhaviṣyatīti saṃbhāvayāmaḥ. yasmāt

yuktiśabdau purā 'py asya na ced akurutāṃ pramām
sākṣād āvartanāt tābhyāṃ kim apūrvaṃ phaliṣyati (124)

athaivam api prasaṃkhyānam antareṇa prāṇān dhārayituṃ na śaknoṣīti cec chravaṇādāv eva saṃpādayiṣyāmaḥ. kathaṃ

prasaṃkhyānaṃ śrutāv asya nyāuo 'stv āmreḍanātmakaḥ
īṣacchrutaṃ sāmisrutaṃ samyak śrutvāvagacchati (125)

nanu prasaṃkhyānavidhim anabhyupagacchataḥ pāramahaṃsī caryā bauddhādicaryāvad aśāstrapūrvikā prāpnoti tataś cārūḍhapatitatvaṃ syād aśeṣakarmaṇāṃ ca nivṛttir na prāpnotīti. ucyate

tvamarthasyāvabodhāya vidhir apy āśrito yataḥ
tam antareṇa ye doṣās te 'pi nāyānty ahetavaḥ (126)

CHAPTER FOUR

caturtho 'dhyāyaḥ

oṃ pūrvādhyāyeṣu yad vastu vistareṇoditaṃ sphuṭam।
saṃkṣepato 'dhunā vakṣye tadevasukhavittaye (1)

saṃkṣepavistarābhyāṃ hi mandottamadhiyāṃ nṛṇām
vastūcyamānam ety antaḥkaraṇaṃ tena bhaṇyate (2)

ātmānātmā ca loke 'smin pratyakṣādipramāṇataḥ
siddhas tayor anātma tu sarvatraivātmapūrvakaḥ (3)

anātmatvaṃ svatas siddhaṃ dehād bhinnasya vastunaḥ
jñātur apy ātmatā tadvan madhye saṃśayadarśanam (4)

asādhāraṇāṃs tayor dharmān jñātvā dhūmāgnivad budhaḥ
anātmano 'tha buddhyantān jānīyād anumānataḥ (5)

idam ity eva bāhye 'rthe hy aham ity eva boddhari
dvayaṃ dṛṣṭaṃ yato dehe tenāyaṃ muhyate janaḥ (6)

kena punar nyāyenātmānātmanor aśvamahiṣayor iva vibhāgaḥ kriyata iti. ucyate

nyāyaḥ purodito 'smābhir ātmānātmavibhāgakṛt
tenedamartham utsārya hy aham ity atra yo bhavet (7)

vidyāt tat tvam asmād bhāvābhāvadṛśaṃ sadā
anantaram abāhyārthaṃ pratyaksthaṃ munir añjasā (8)

ucyatāṃ tarhi kayā tu paripāṭhyā vākyārthaṃ vettīti. ucyate. anvayavyatirekābhyām

tyaktakṛtsnedam arthatvāt tyakto 'ham iti manyate
nāvagacchāmy ahaṃ yasmān nijātmānam anātmanaḥ (9)

atha śarīrādibuddhiparyantaḥ sa sarvo 'nātmaiveti pramāṇād viniścitya kim iti bubhutsāto noparamate śṛṇu

anucchinnabubhutsas ca pratyagg hetor anātmanaḥ
dolāyamānacitto 'yaṃ muhyate bhautavan naraḥ (10)

aviluptavijñānātmana ātmatvād eva nityasānnidhyād bubhutsuḥ kim iti na pratipadyata iti. yasmāt

yair adrākṣīt purātmānaṃ yam anātmeti vīkṣate
dṛṣṭer draṣṭāram ātmānaṃ taiḥ prasiddhaiḥ pramitsati (11)

kasmāt punar hetoḥ parācīnābhiḥ śabdādyavalehinībhir buddhibhir ātmānam anātmavan na vīkṣata iti. ucyate

cakṣur na vīkṣate śabdam atadātmatvakāraṇat
yathaivaṃ bhautika dṛṣṭir nātmānaṃ paripaśyati (12)

pratyakṣādipramāṇasvābhāvyānurodhena tāvat tadadarśanakāraṇam uktam. atha prameyasvābhāvyānurodhena pratiṣedha ucyate

dhīvikriyāsahasrāṇāṃ hānopādānadharmiṇām
sadā sākṣiṇam ātmānaṃ pratyaktvān nāham īkṣate (13)

kva punar iyaṃ vivekabuddhiḥ kim ātmany utānātmanīti. kiṃcātaḥ. yady ātmani kūṭasthatvavyāghāto 'nātmadarśitvāt. athānātmani tasyāpy acaitanyān na vivekasaṃbandha iti. ucyate. "dāhyadāhakataikatra" ity uktaparihārāt

buddhāv eva viveko 'yaṃ yadanātmatayā bhidā
buddhim evopamṛdnāti kadalīṃ tatphalaṃ yathā (14)

so 'yam atattve tattvadṛk

anumānapradīpena hitvā sarvān anātmanaḥ
saṃsāraikāvalambinyā tadabhāvaṃ dhiyepsati (15)

yo 'yam anvayavyatirekajo viveka ātmānātma-vibhāgalakṣaṇo 'nātmasthaḥ sthāṇau saṃśayāvabodhavat pratipattavyo 'yathāvastusvābhāvyān mṛgatṛṣṇikodaka-prabodhavad ity ata āha

saṃsārabījasaṃstho 'yaṃ taddhiyā muktim icchati
śaśo nimīlaneneva mṛtyuṃ parijihīrṣati (16)

asyārthasya draḍhimne śrutyudāharaṇam

imam arthaṃ puraskṛtya śrutyā samyag udāhṛtam
"yac cakṣuṣe" ti visrabdhaṃ "na dṛṣṭe" riti ca sphuṭam (17)

buddhyantam apaviddhyaivaṃ ko nvahaṃ syām itīkṣituḥ
śrutis tat tvam asīty āha sarvamānātigāminī (18)

eṣa saṃkṣepataḥ pūrvādhyāyatrayasyārtha uktaḥ. so 'yaṃ nyāyyo 'pi vedāntārthaḥ śāstrācāryaprasādalabhyo 'py anapekṣitaśāstrācāryaprasādo 'nanyāpekṣasiddha svabhāva-tvāt kaiścic chraddadhānair na pratīyate. teṣāṃ saṃgrahārtham abhimataprāmāṇyodāharaṇam

bhagavatpūjyapādaiś cāpy udāhāryevaṃ eva tu
suvispaṣṭo 'smadukto 'rthaḥ sarvabhūtahitaiṣibhiḥ (19)

kiṃ paramātmana upadeśa utāparamātmana iti. kiṃ cātaḥ. yadi paramātmanas tasyopadeśam antareṇaiva muktatvān nirarthaka upadeśaḥ. athāparamātmanas tasyāpi svata eva saṃsārasvabhāvatvān niṣphala upadeśaḥ. evam ubhayatrāpi doṣavattvād ata āha

"avivicyobhayaṃ vakti śrutiś cet syā grahas tathā"
iti pakṣam upādāya pūrvapakṣam niśātya ca (20)

tac cedam avivekāt svato viviktātmane tat tvam asīty upadiṣṭam

yuṣmadasmadvibhāgajñe syād arthavad itaṃ vacaḥ
yato 'nabhijñe vākyaṃ syād badhireṣv iva gāyanaṃ (21)

tasya ca yuṣmadasmadvibhāgavijñānasya kā yuktir upāyabhāvaṃ pratipadyate śṛṇu

"anvayavyatirekau hi padārthasya padasya ca
syād etad aham ity atra yuktir evāvadhāraṇe (22)

kathaṃ tau yluktir ity atrāha

"nādrākṣam ahaṃ ity asmin suṣupte 'nyan manāg api
na vārayati dṛṣṭiṃ svāṃ pratyayaṃ tu niṣedhati" (23)

"evaṃ vijñātavācyārthe śrutilokaprasiddhitaḥ
śrutis tat tvam asīty āha śrotur mohāpanuttaye" (24)

tatra tvam iti padaṃ yatra lakṣaṇayā vartate so 'rtha ucyate

"ahaṃśabdasya yā niṣṭhā jyotiṣi pratyagātmani
saivoktā sad asīty evaṃ phalaṃ tatra vimuktatā" (25)

anyaccānvayavyatirekodāharaṇam. tathā

"chittvā tyaktena hastena svayaṃ nātmā viśeṣyate
tathā śiṣṭena sarveṇa yena yena viśeṣyate (26)

viśeṣaṇam idaṃ sarvaṃ sādhvalaṃkaraṇaṃ yathā
avidyādhyastam ataḥ sarvaṃ jñāta ātmany asad bhavet (27)

tasmāt tyaktena hastena tulyaṃ sarvaṃ viśeṣaṇam
anātmatvena tasmāj kño muktaḥ sarvaviśeṣaṇaiḥ (28)

jñātaivātmā sadā grāhyo jñeyam utsṛiya kevalaḥ
aham ity api yad grāhyaṃ vyapetāṅgasamaṃ hi tat (29)

dṛśyatvād aham ity eṣa nātmadharmo ghaṭādivat
tathānye pratyayā jñeyā doṣāś cātmā 'malo hy ataḥ (30)

sarvanyāyopasaṃgrahaḥ

"nityamuktatvavijñānaṃ vākyād bhavati nānyataḥ
vākyārthasyāpi vijñānaṃ padārthasmṛtipūrvakam (31)

anvayavyatirekābhyāṃ padārthas smaryate dhruvam
evaṃ nirduḥkham ātmānam akriyaṃ pratipadyate (32)

sad evetyādivākyebhyaḥ pramā sphuṭatarā bhavet
daśamas tvam asīty asmād yathaivaṃ pratyagātmani" (33)

vīkṣāpannasyodāharaṇam

"navabuddhyapahārādd hi svātmānaṃ daśapūraṇam
apaśyan jñātum evecchet svam ātmānaṃ janas tathā (34)

avidyābaddha cakṣuṣṭvāt kāmāpahṛtadhīḥ sadā
viviktaṃ dṛśim ātmānaṃ nekṣate daśamaṃ yathā" (35)

so 'yam evam avidyāpaṭalāvaguṇṭhitadṛṣṭiḥ san katham utthāpyata ity āha

yathā svāpanimittena svapnadṛkpratibodhitaḥ
karaṇaṃ karma kartāraṃ svāpnaṃ naivekṣate svataḥ (36)

anātmajñas tathaivāyaṃ samyak śrutyāvabodhitaḥ
guruṃ śāstraṃ tathā mūḍhaṃ svātmano 'nyaṃ na paśyati (37)

sa kiṃ sakalasaṃsārapraviviktam ātmānaṃ vākyāt pratipadyata uta netīti. atra brūmaḥ. kūṭasthāvagatiśeṣamātratvāt pratipatter ata āha

daṇḍāvasānaniṣṭhas syād daṇḍasarpo yathā tathā
nityāvagatiniṣṭhaṃ syād vākyāj jagad asaṃśayam (38)

kuta etat. yasmāt

pasyann iti yadāhoccaiḥ pratyaktvam ajam avyayam
apūrvānaparānantaṃ tvamā tad upalakṣyate (39)

tattvamasyādivākyotthavijñānenaiva bādhyate. yasmāt

asmād yad aparaṃ rūpaṃ nāstīty eva nirūpyate
anyathāgrahaṇābhāvād bījaṃ tat svapnabodhayoḥ (40)

asyārthasya draḍhimna udāharaṇam

"kāryakāraṇabaddhau tāv iṣyete viśvataijasau
prājñaḥ kāraṇabaddhas tu dvau tau turye na sidhyataḥ" (41)

"anyathāgrhṇataḥ svapno nidrā tattvam ajānataḥ
viparyāse tayoḥ kṣīṇe turīyaṃ padam aśnute" (42)

tathā bhagavatpādīyam udāharaṇam

"suṣuptākhyaṃ tamo 'jñānaṃ bījaṃ svapnaprabodhayoḥ
ātmabodhapradagdhaṃ syād bījaṃ dagdhaṃ yathā 'bhavam" (43)

evaṃ gauḍair drāviḍair naḥ pūjyair ayam arthaḥ prabhāṣitaḥ
ajñānamātropādhis sann ahamādidṛgīśvaraḥ (44)

tatrānyathāgrahaṇavad anyathāgrahaṇabījam agrahaṇam anātmadharma evety āha

idaṃ jñānam ahaṃ jñātā jñeyam etad iti trayam
yo 'vikāro vijānāti parāg evāsya tat tamaḥ (45)

yata etad evam atas tasyaiva bījātmanas tamasaś cittadharmaviśiṣṭasya svakāryadvitīyābhisaṃbandho na tv avikāriṇa ātmana ity āha dṛṣṭāntena

rūpaprakāśayor yadvat saṃgatir vikriyāvataḥ
sukhaduḥkhādisaṃbandhaś cittasyaivaṃ vikāriṇaḥ (46)

tad etad anvayavyatirekābhyāṃ darśayiṣyam āha

saṃprasāde 'vikāritvād astaṃ yāte vikāriṇi
paśyato nātmanaḥ kiṃcid dvitīyaṃ spṛśate 'ṇv api (47)

so 'yaṃ kūṭasthajñānamūrtir ātmā

yathā prājñe tathaivāyaṃ svapnajāgaritāntayoḥ
paśyann apy avikāritvād dvitīyaṃ naiva paśyati (48)

evaṃ jñānavato nāsti mamāhaṃmatisaṃśrayaḥ
bhāsvatpradīpahastasya hy andhakāra ivāgrataḥ (49)

tatra dṛṣṭāntaḥ

ā prabodhād yathā 'siddhir dvaitād anyasya vastunaḥ
bodhād evam asiddhatvaṃ buddhyādeḥ pratyagātmanaḥ
(50)

sa eṣa vidvān hānopādānaśūnyam ātmānam ātmani paśyan

sarvam evānujānāti sarvam eva niṣedhati
bhedātmalābho 'nujñā syān niṣedho 'tatsvabhāvataḥ (51)

sarvasyoktatvād upasaṃhāraḥ

paramārthātmaniṣṭhaṃ yat sarvavedāntaniścitam
tamopanud dhiyāṃ jñānaṃ tad etat kathitaṃ mayā (52)

etāvadihoktam

nehātmavin madanyo 'sti na matto 'jño 'sti kaścana
ity ajānan vijānāti yas sa brahmavid uttamaḥ (53)

evam ātmānaṃ jñātvā kiṃ pravartitavyam uta nivartitavyam āhosvin muktapragrahateti. ucyate

jñeyābhinnam idaṃ yasmāj jñeyavastvanusāryataḥ
na pravṛttiṃ nivṛttiṃ vā kaṭākṣeṇāpi vīkṣate (54)

kuta etajñeyābhinnam iti. yataḥ

prāgātmabodhād bodho 'yaṃ bāhyavastūpasarjanaḥ
pradhvastākhilasaṃsāra ātmaikālambanaḥ śruteḥ (55)

evam avagataparamārthatattvasya na śeṣaśeṣibhāvas tatkāraṇasyotsāritatvād ity āha

vāstavenaiva vṛttena niruṇaddhi yato bhavam
nivṛttim api mṛdnāti samyagbodhaḥ pravṛttivat (56)

sakṛd ātmaprasūtyaiva niruṇaddhy akhilaṃ bhavam
dhvāntamātranirāsena na tato 'nyānyathāmatiḥ (57)

deśakālādyasaṃbaddhād deśāder mohakāryataḥ
nānutpannam adagdhaṃ vā jñānam ajñānam asty ataḥ (58)

samyagjñānaśikhipluṣṭamohatatkāryarūpiṇaḥ
sakṛn nivṛtter bādhyasya kiṃ kāryam avaśiṣyate (59)

vāstavenaiva vṛttenāvidyāyāḥ pradhvastatvān na kiṃcid avaśiṣyata ity uktaḥ parihāraḥ. athāparas sāmpradāyikaḥ

nivṛttasarpas sarpotthaṃ yathā kampaṃ na muñcati
vidhvastākhilamoho 'pi mohakāryaṃ tathātmavit (60)

yataḥ pravṛttibījam ucchinnaṃ tasmāt

taror utkhātamūlasya śoṣeṇaiva yathā kṣayaḥ
tathā buddhātmatattvasya nivṛttyaiva tanukṣayaḥ (61)

athālepakapakṣanirāsārtham āha

buddhādvaitasatattvasya yatheṣṭācaraṇaṃ yadi
śunāṃ tattvadṛśāṃ caiva ko bhedo 'śucibhakṣaṇe (62)

kasmān na bhavati. yasmāt

adharmāj jāyate 'jñānaṃ yatheṣṭācaraṇaṃ tataḥ
dharmakārye kathaṃ tat syād yatra dharmo 'pi neṣyate (63)

pratyācakṣāṇa āhāto yatheṣṭācaraṇaṃ hariḥ
"yasya sarve samārambhāḥ" "prakāśaṃ ce" ti sarvadṛk (64)

tiṣṭhatu tāvat sarvapravṛttibījaghasmaraṃ jñānaṃ mumukṣyavasthāyām api na saṃbhavati yatheṣṭācaraṇaṃ. tad āha

"yo hi yatra viraktaḥ syān nāsau tasmai pravartate
lokatrayaviraktatvān mumukṣuḥ kim itīhate" (65)

tatra dṛṣṭāntaḥ

"kṣudhayā pīḍyamāno 'pi na viṣaṃ hy attum icchati
miṣṭānnadhvastatṛḍ jānan nāmūḍhas taj jighatsati (66)

yato 'vagataparamārthatattvasya yatheṣṭācaraṇaṃ na manāg api ghaṭate mumukṣutve 'pi ca tasmāt

rāgo liṅgam abodhasya cittavyāyāmabhūmiṣu
kutaḥ śādvalatā tasya yasyāgniḥ koṭare taroḥ (67)

sakalapuruṣārthasamāptikāriṇo 'syātmāvabodhasya kutaḥ prasūtir iti. ucyate

amānitvādiniṣṭo yo yaś cādveeṣṭrādisādhanaḥ
jñānam utpadyate tasya na bahirmukhacetasaḥ (68)

utpanna ātmavijñāne kim avidyākāryatvāt pravṛttivan nivṛttyātmakāmānitvādayo nivartanta uta neti. neti brūmaḥ. kiṃ kāraṇam. nivṛttiśāstrāviruddhasvābhāvyāt paramātmano na tu niyogavaśāt. kathaṃ tarhi. śṛṇu

utpannātmaprabodhasya tv adveṣṭṛtvādayo guṇāḥ
ayatnato bhavanty asya na tu sādhanarūpiṇaḥ (69)

yata etad evam ataḥ

imaṃ grantham upāditsur amānitvādisādhanaḥ
yatnataḥ syān na durvṛttaḥ pratyagdharmānugo hy ayam (70)

na dātavyaś cāyaṃ granthaḥ

nāviraktāya saṁsārān nānirastaiṣaṇāya ca
na cāyamavate deyaṃ vedāntārthapraveśanam (71)

jñātvā yathoditaṃ samyag jñātavyaṃ nāvaśiṣyate
na cānirastakarmedaṃ jānīyād añjasā tataḥ (72)

nirastasarvakarmāṇaḥ pratyakpravaṇabuddhayaḥ
niṣkāmā yatayaḥ śāntā jānantīdaṃ yathoditam (73)

śrīmacchaṅkarapādapadmayugalaṃ
saṃsevya labdhvocivān
jñānaṃ pāramahaṃsyam etad amalaṃ
svāntāndhakārāpanut
mā bhūd atra virodhinī matir ataḥ
sadbhiḥ parīkṣyaṃ budhaiḥ

sarvatraiva viśuddhaye matam idaṃ
santaḥ paraṃ kāraṇam (74)

subhāṣitaṃ cārv api nāmahātmanāṃ
divākaro naktadṛśām ivāmalaḥ
prabhāti bhāty eva viśuddhacetasāṃ
nidhir yathāpāstatṛṣāṃ mahādhanaḥ (75)

viṣṇoḥ pādānugāṃ yāṃ nikhilabhavanudaṃ
śaṃkaro 'vāpa yogāt
sarvajñaṃ brahmasaṃsthaṃ munigaṇasahitaṃ
samyag abhyarcya bhaktyā
vidyāṃ gaṅgām ivāhaṃ pravaraguṇanidheḥ
prāpya vedānta dīptāṃ
kāruṇyāt tām avocaṃ janimṛtinivaha
dhvastaye duḥkhitebhyaḥ (76)

vedāntodaravarti bhāsvad amalaṃ
dhvāntacchid asmad dhiyo
divyaṃ jñānam atīndriye 'pi viṣaye
vyāhanyate na kvacit
yo no nyāyaśalākayaivanikhilaṃ
saṃsārabījaṃ tamaḥ
protsāryāvirakārṣīd guruguruḥ
pūjyāya tasmai namaḥ (77)